WHEN I SAY MOVE....

WHEN I SAY MOVE....

STEWART R. DINNEN

CHRISTIAN LITERATURE CRUSADE

CHRISTIAN LITERATURE CRUSADE
The Dean, Alresford, Hants.

U.S.A.
Box C, Fort Washington, Pennsylvania 19034.

AUSTRALIA
Box 91, Pennant Hills, N.S.W. 2120.

NEW ZEALAND
Box 1688, Auckland, C.1.

also in

Europe, Canada,
Central America, South America,
West Indies, Africa, India,
Indonesia, Far East

Printed in England by Plowprint, London, SE18 7JH

Foreword

WHERE the Holy Spirit is in action through any member of Christ's body, there is freshness, originality and daring in the fulfilment of some great purpose. It is not the importance, dignity or efficiency of the agent that strikes the observer, but just one fact: "Here is God at work." That was so in our Worldwide Evangelization Crusade when C. T. Studd started out alone for the heart of Africa over fifty years ago. Either this was a crazy man, or it was the Holy Spirit reaching unreached millions in a way which all men would recognise as God's power through man's weakness.

Fifty years, forty fields, twelve hundred in the two Crusades (W.E.C. and Christian Literature Crusade), tens of thousands who have confessed Christ, national churches with their own national leaders, literature centres worldwide—these are evidences that it was God. But after fifty years? Is it a living missionary organism hardening into yet another "organization"?

My delight in this contemporary witness by Stewart Dinnen is that here is the answer. If W.E.C. were now more concerned with organized respectability, or considered academic standards more important for new recruits than the Spirit-filled equipment of Acts 1:8, then it would stick out its ugly head in no uncertain way in this detailed record. But it doesn't. Thank God! Here is the man who has been the Principal of our two Missionary Training Centres. He has the academic background and experience in a commissioned rank of the British Army in World War II. But that is not what stands out. I find the story of a man who himself first went through God's mill "which grinds exceeding small", and took the grinding, until Christ and the world's need of Him became his meat and drink in place of self-interest. I find him then, together with

vii

Marie his wife, walking boldly that way which appears absurd, the way of faith where the unreachable is continually being reached, not by appeals to man, but by appropriating the resources of God; and thus by going that way themselves and living it, are able to train others. They and their staff give the best of academic and practical missionary and evangelistic training, so that every available talent can be put to full use for God; not in order to turn out graduates of a Training College with bigger heads than hearts, but humble, dedicated young men and women, crucified, risen and ascended with Christ. Their aim is to produce those who have individually proved in practical living the faithfulness of God, and who have taken at least the first steps in the life of prevailing prayer, effective soul-winning, and preparation for years of loving identification with the peoples of the countries to which they are called, not as superiors, but as servants for Jesus' sake.

I have known, loved, and been in close contact with Stewart and Marie since they first came as recruits to W.E.C. before they were married, and since then as co-leaders of our British and European Missionary Training Centre in Glasgow, and now as leaders of our Australian and New Zealand Training Centre in Tasmania. If this was a story of facts and figures, it would weary me; but it is the thrill of a great adventure, *the* great adventure, the miracle God-led life which turns the most humdrum into that true excitement, the combination of an intense seriousness with an inner core of gaiety—"Who for the joy set before Him, endured the cross."

NORMAN P. GRUBB

International Secretary Emeritus of the
Worldwide Evangelization Crusade.

Philadelphia
December 1970

Preface

THERE have been a number of requests that our testimony should be published. A few days of enforced rest due to a damaged knee seemed to be the ideal time to commence the manuscript, and with the subsequent help, advice, and encouragement of a number of colleagues and friends worldwide, this book has been prepared.

My wife, Marie, and I became staff members of the Missionary Training College of the Worldwide Evangelization Crusade in Glasgow, Scotland, in 1949. Eight years later we were transferred to our American Headquarters at Fort Washington, Pennsylvania, and in 1960, owing to certain difficulties that had arisen at the Crusade's Training College in Tasmania, we were asked to join the Australian staff and take charge of this developing project.

An account of our earlier experience in Britain is included in Elsie Rowbotham's book *Would You Believe It!* (published by W.E.C., London).

Apart from the glimpses in retrospect that comprise most of the first two chapters, this book is our testimony of proving God over the past eleven years in Australia.

A word of explanation. The commencement of the Missionary Training College at St. Leonards, Tasmania, in 1956 came after the purchase of a forty-five acre property known as "Tolarno". This was made possible by a number of large designated gifts from local interested friends. The project was the vision of Arthur Davidson, the Australian secretary of

W.E.C. at that time. It was initiated in Tasmania by Mr. Colin Haynes, now of Shepparton, Victoria, and the first Principal, from 1957 to 1960, was the Rev. J. L. Lincolne, now of Latrobe, Tasmania.

The present staff are ten in number and the student body is sixty-one; there are forty-one Australians, eighteen New Zealanders and two South Africans.

I would like to acknowledge with appreciation the help of those who took part in the compiling of the story: my wife, whose records and files of correspondence with graduates provided much valuable material; Norman Grubb and Dr. Irl Duling in U.S.A.; Jock Purves in Scotland and Esma Harris in Sydney who made valuable detailed suggestions after reading the manuscript; and Florence Smith of W.E.C. Headquarters in England who cared for a host of details as secretary of the W.E.C. publications committee.

STEWART R. DINNEN

St. Leonards,
Tasmania.
July 1971

Contents

						Page
	Foreword	...	...	...	...	...	vii
	Preface	...	...	...	...	...	xi
1.	Moving	...	...	...	...	...	13
2.	Learning	...	...	...	...	...	19
3.	Building	...	...	...	...	...	30
4.	Developing	...	...	...	...	...	36
5.	Training	...	...	...	...	...	47
6.	Spreading	...	...	...	...	...	56
7.	Journeying	...	...	...	...	...	67
8.	Fruitbearing	...	...	...	...	...	76
9.	Timing	...	...	...	...	...	85
10.	Expounding	...	...	...	...	...	95
	Backdrop—Tasmania		...	...	...	...	107

1

Moving

"AND when I say 'MOVE'," said this mass of human flesh, our army P.T. Instructor—the nearest thing to confounding my opposition to the evolution theory —"when I say 'MOVE' . . . I don't want you to WALK . . . and I don't want you to RUN . . . I want you to . . . FLY!"

We flew.

We flew because we knew we had to please him, and keep on pleasing him. Of course it was a compulsive obedience based on fear, but the incident has stuck so vividly in my mind since July 1942, because of the sheer simplicity of it. Just OBEY. That's all that matters.

I am amazed when I challenge young Christians today with the thrust—"Are you sure you are in the will of God?"—that so few can answer right off with a joyous smile and a confident certainty.

Four years passed after the above incident—two years of being licked into shape by other well-meaning but uncouth sergeants, and two years of "productive" army service that took me from radar maintenance on an anti-aircraft site in Manchester to the duties of Adjutant of Malaya Command Signals, Kuala Lumpur.

Demobbed, free and questioning, I stood on a snow-covered hill near Aberfoyle in my native Scotland, facing out this fundamental issue of obedience.

Christ as Saviour? Yes! Ever since that Sunday afternoon when James Meiklejohn of Scripture Union

13

spoke to me about Christ as we came out of Jordanhill Crusader Bible Class. I walked home slowly weighing the odds, and eventually, finding the house full of visitors and a bridge party in progress, I went to the only quiet spot available—the bathroom. Kneeling by the bath, I asked the Saviour to save me. And He did. I proved the reality of His presence all through school, university and the army. But Christ as Lord? The answer to that was wobbly. Sometimes it had been "yes" but more often it had been "not now, Lord".

But this time I was cornered. I had just listened to Dr. Wilfred Morris of India. It was not the message which challenged, it was the man, speaking out of a life-time of service for Christ in India, and I knew I was being asked to yield totally to the will of God. Would this lead back to India for me, too?

India! What memories! The first ten miserable days when the tummy tried hard to adjust to the change in food, and one never strayed more than fifty yards from the facilities of barracks. Then the order to take two hundred sepoys half-way across the continent without knowing a word of their language. Burma and the forgotten army. ("Forgotten?" our Supreme Commander, Mountbatten, had said. "They haven't forgotten you: they've never even heard of you!") The rain . . . rain . . . rain. The impoverished Burmese . . . the abject Japanese . . . the starving British prisoners flown into Rangoon at the end of hostilities. Malaya, and the material and spiritual need of the youth whom one had come to love. Excusing myself (as Detachment Commander!) from Army duties for an hour each day, there had been the priceless privilege of teaching in a mission school. Memories of what? Need . . . need . . . need . . . And I knew that, logically anyway, to yield to the Lordship of Christ would mean . . . (that word again) "MOVE!" And probably move to an

14

underdeveloped area where "need" clamoured from every village. "Why should anyone hear of Christ twice while some have never heard of Him once?" a Canadian preacher had asked, and the logic of it was unanswerable.

"All right, Lord."

It was as simple as that, but it has carried a lifetime of meaning ever since.

Instead of that professional security for which I was shortly to qualify ("Surely You need Christian high school teachers, Lord!") it was back to the training level again. Instead of the new car my folks had promised on demobilisation, it was a push bicycle. Instead of the steady wage packet, it meant using up that hoarded officer's pay and, when that was finished (and He saw to it that it diminished pretty quickly), it meant trusting the Lord. Later, even the carefully hoarded fees for the second year at the Missionary Training College were needed to help send a new missionary to India in a hurry. But the good Lord supplied in another way, plus six pounds sterling for good measure—you can't beat God at giving!

My, what a topsy turvy business this life of naked faith-and-obedience is, "having nothing, yet possessing all things", being challenged to surrender on some issue, then finding God "making it up" and adding a blessing for good measure!

When Stewart Dinnen met a lovely young nurse called Marie Gourdie the friendship developed marvellously—for a while. But there was deep uncertainty regarding God's purpose for my life. The Cross had to come across this friendship until in God's good time the issue of guidance was crystal clear to both of us, and we knew we could go ahead in God's perfect will. We were married in August 1948.

The Lord took the captain's hoard already mentioned, but we have lived on the Lord's plenty for nearly twenty-five years.

We left life in the homeland where we were surrounded by dozens of friends, only to make a host of new ones in the service of the Lord, in Canada, U.S.A., New Zealand and Australia.

We surrendered the possibility of a larger family in early married years for the sake of the work, but now, as well as our two natural daughters, we have spiritual sons and daughters—those we have helped train—in thirty countries round the world. We exchanged good prospects in professional fields for one of the most challenging and rewarding ministries—the responsibility for the preparation of young people for Christian service. No. You just can't beat God at giving!

The will of the Lord . . . what was it to mean after that encounter with Him on a Scottish hillside? It turned out to mean two-and-a-half years of missionary and Bible training, first for a term at Lebanon Missionary College at Berwick in the North of England, and then in Glasgow, living at the Scottish Headquarters of W.E.C., travelling each day to lectures at the Evangelical Baptist Fellowship Bible College. Packed days, glorious days, enriching days. And the fun! Who could forget George, who always went to sleep in the mid-afternoon study period, waking up once to find desks, books and writing gear removed by practical jokers? Or Geoff, who rounded up and hid every razor the night before end of term so that every male student went home grizzly and unkempt? Or Sandy, trying to be impressive in the missionary meeting and pleading for a heathen country where there were 25,000 missionaries to every native and where these poor people were dying like flies going to a lost eternity? Or the tongue-tied lady student in the open-air meeting who cried, "I am a man and no worm"? Or Isobel in her dedicated spinsterhood who, in the prayer time, burdened for the need of men missionaries in a certain area of Colombia cried, "And Lord, send a man for Mitu (me too!)."

The leaders of W.E.C. in Scotland were Fran and Elsie Rowbotham. They were business people whom God called out of Birmingham to Colombia and from there guided them into the home-base activities of the Crusade. What a job they had with us! But how we learned from them, not only by what they said, but from how they lived before us and loved us and believed. What lessons of faith and tolerance towards us hot-headed youngsters!

But beyond training—what was the will of God? Marie and I had been burdened for W.E.C. and India and felt we should head towards it after graduation. As the end of College days came in sight, however, there was a distinct inner witness that this was not to be. Instead came an increasing burden for the new training programme developing around Fran and Elsie. But how could this work out? We committed it to God.

Three things happened. First, in an evening of prayer together the remark was passed that, instead of the young man at present at Cambridge who had planned to join the teaching staff, but who was now withdrawing, perhaps God already had His chosen ones IN THE MIDST. Secondly, when Norman Grubb came to Scotland to discuss Mission matters, he raised the very issue of our staying at home for a time. Thirdly, in a weekend of fasting and prayer, we came through to full assurance on this issue.

Later as candidates at W.E.C. Headquarters we secretly asked God for one more sign—a gift of £1,000 towards the extension of the Missionary Training College property. The day before we left Headquarters a letter was placed in our hands with the promise of £1,000 towards the development of the new M.T.C.! At first we thought it was a hoax, but sure enough, some weeks later on return to London after a short holiday, there was the cheque—a bank cheque so arranged that the donor might remain anonymous.

2

Learning

SO we came on the staff of the newly constituted W.E.C. Missionary Training College in Glasgow, "just for a year's experiment" as the Mission put it. The year's experiment lasted for eight years—eight years in which we learnt much more than we taught! For we saw God work in line with the "naked" faith-and-obedience pattern lived before us by our senior workers.

Immediately after we were married we lived in one room containing only the barest essentials. We had been given enough money as wedding presents to furnish it well and planned to do so gradually. However, one day a load of second-hand beds for the College arrived, to be paid for on delivery. We knew there just wasn't enough ready cash in the office to cover it, and the Lord told us to use our wedding present money.

"But this is all we have, Lord, and our folks will want to see us fixed up nicely. . . . We need this."

"Freely ye have received. Freely give."

We obeyed. Within twenty-four hours someone came on the phone and said, "Have you purchased a bedroom suite yet?"

"Well . . . we've been thinking about it . . ."

"Go ahead and get one—a good one—and send me the bill."

Hallelujah!

And who can forget the succession of young men

and women who passed through the school and on into vital and strategic service? Tom, who became field leader even before his first term was up. Kees, who was described by a missionary statesman as one of the most vital missionaries he had met in his whole tour of the Orient. June, who later received highest commendation from the Bible Society for the standard of her New Testament translation into a Liberian language. Jim Rodger, who gave his life standing alongside his fellow missionary in the hellish nightmare of the Congo crisis. Or Helen and Alistair and their most strategic ministry to the whole of the French-speaking student world of West and Central Africa? Or Andrew, that spiritual dare-devil, who as "God's Smuggler" still runs a scarlet pimpernel ministry behind the Iron Curtain? Wonderful people—but only because of a wonderful Saviour released to work through them on the basis of simple faith-and-obedience.

During these years God spoke about another little bit of obedience. "Go to America and take the course offered by the Summer Institute of Linguistics at Oklahoma University so that you will be better equipped to help students face their future language hurdles." Three hundred miles away a keen Christian doctor who had come to hear of our interest in linguistics through a missionary on deputation, wrote and said, "I'm conscious of the battles many missionaries face in language, and I want to help you to have the benefit of this course in America. I'm selling my motor cycle and the proceeds will help with your fare."

So we had our fares, one way. On applying for visas, however, the U.S. Consul told us that we could not obtain these until our return fares were paid and tickets produced in evidence. No waifs and strays to be left hanging round Uncle Sam's belt, thank you!

So we prayed but nothing happened. . . . Until

the day that Leonore arrived en route from Africa to Canada on furlough.

"Stewart, run me down to the travel agent so I can book a passage to Vancouver."

"Sure."

(En route to the city.) "By the way, do you have the money?"

"Of course not, but by the time the reservations come through the Lord will have supplied."

I gulped, and later as I stood behind her in the travel agency I marvelled at the certainty of her faith.

"Go thou and do likewise," said a voice in my heart.

"Oh no, Lord, I've never done anything like this."

"Ask the clerk to try for shipping reservations to Canada."

Leonore completed her business and I nervously approached the clerk. . . .

When we finally returned to Headquarters I was immediately called to the office. "Someone has just handed this in to help you with your transatlantic fares." There was a cheque which covered the remaining amount necessary to complete our round-trip fares. Faith **and** obedience! This lesson of the "launch of faith" has never left us.

But how were we to live in Canada-U.S.A. for six months for a familiarisation tour of other Bible Institutes as well as the Linguistics course when currency restrictions made it impossible to take money out of Britain?

Two more miracles saw us through. Through a meeting with Dr. Kenneth Pike, a director of Wycliffe Bible Translators who "happened" to be passing through Glasgow en route to a conference in Norway, we were offered the course free of cost. (We subsequently showed our appreciation by teaching in the newly-formed British Summer Institute of Linguistics for several years.) Then we heard that Charlie Searle, the director of our Missionary Children's Home in Scotland who was in America for a series of meetings, was shortly returning, bringing several large gifts of money donated by American friends for the work of the Home. Simultaneously, other gifts started to arrive for our tour. Solution? Simply ask Charlie to leave behind at our U.S. Headquarters the equivalent in dollars to the sterling amounts given to us in the U.K., and we remit this to the Children's Home in Arbroath. There are no problems with God.

So we travelled 10,000 miles. We visited many Bible Institutes, as well as the W.E.C. Headquarters in Canada, Chicago and Philadelphia, and survived the twelve-week course in the searing heat of Oklahoma, courtesy of S.I.L. Through a forwarding agency we were even able to pick up a new car in Detroit and drive it to its purchaser near Oklahoma City, receiving payment for services rendered, on delivery!

Our visit had long-term repercussions. A close link was established with the North American W.E.C. staff, some of whom liked the idea of having their own special training school, and in 1957 we were invited to join them with a view to establishing some kind of centre to be run on similar lines to those developing in Glasgow.

Was this invitation in the will of the Lord? We went to prayer and the Scripture which spoke clearly was I Sam. 10: 7, "Do as occasion serve thee" ("Do whatever you find to be done"—Amplified Bible).

But could we leave the College? Some time before this, the Lord in His gracious planning had directed into our two-year training course a young man with a most interesting background. Bill Chapman held a B.A. from Oxford University and had had

Army experience overseas. He had caught the vision of true discipleship, and a wealthy home background could not deter him from entering into the simple faith-walk of the Crusade. It became clear to Bill and the staff that it was God's purpose for him to join us, so after the orientation course for new candidates in London, he commenced teaching at the college. With Bill preparing to take over as the new Director of Studies, the British staff of W.E.C. were willing to release us for North America.

It was one thing to trust God when surrounded by friends, but what would happen in U.S.A. where we knew only a few fellow-workers, and to which no one in Britain, because of currency restrictions, could send us money?

What a rebuke later awaited us on this issue! The very day we landed in the United States a Scots friend, whom we'd lost track of when he emigrated four years previously, turned up at our Headquarters a few minutes after we arrived. He and his wife helped us to unpack, then took us off to the local supermarket where they loaded us with groceries, topping that off with a good old U.S. ten dollar bill!

Before we reached our destination, however, there was another confirmation of our obedience being in the will of God. In prayer I asked the Lord for clear guidance on the details of "when" and "how". Quite clearly the instructions were impressed on me, "November 23rd, by air, to Philadelphia."

On enquiry we found that a special concession for emigrants brought the air fare lower than ship! But here our "guidance" seemed to come unstuck.

"Sorry," said the man from Cook's Travel Agency. "There are no through flights to Philadelphia. You can fly to New York—on the 22nd." Crestfallen we told him to go ahead and ask for reservations. Ten days later when I was there again checking up on progress, he said, "Funny thing happened to me on the way home, that day you came in and asked about flying to Philadelphia."

"What was that?"

"The agent for Pan American, a friend of mine, came over and sat beside me on the bus. He asked me if I had any problems, so I told him about you. What do you think he said? 'Pan Am is starting a new weekly flight London-Glasgow-New York-Philadelphia.' The first goes on 16th November so you'll be right for November 23rd, right through to Philadelphia!"

Another miracle of the Lord's supply came through our contact with Mr. C. of Racine, Wisconsin. Our only connection with him was that Marie's brother had been a pen friend of his daughter and we had called on him once during our visit to America in 1952. But it was enough to forge a link. Mr. C. took a great interest in our return to the States five years later and one day, when driving up to New York on business in his Cadillac, he pulled into our Headquarters which is just off the Pennsylvania turnpike, and asked to see us.

"I'm having a problem with my income tax," he said. "It would be a great help to me if I could give away a certain amount of money and thereby bring myself into a lower tax bracket. Would you be willing to accept a gift of $500?"

It didn't take us too long to convince him that we were not embarrassed to say, "Yes!" A few weeks later we had a note from him. "That $500 hasn't brought me low enough yet, so I am sending a further $500!"

Interest in the project of a North American Training Centre for W.E.C. started to grow. During the first two years various large gifts were lodged with the Crusade earmarked for such a purpose, but somehow we never had the clear assurance that God was going to raise up a school on the British pattern. We were asked, pending the development of the North American centre, to take charge of the candidate programme at our Philadelphia Headquarters. We had some very precious experiences in this—not the least being the privilege of helping to orientate some very fine American crusaders, among them one young man named Bill McChesney.

Bill was a "Weccer" at heart before he ever came to the Crusade. Educated at a Christian school in Phoenix, Arizona, with a solid Christian home background, he did missionary training at the Great Commission School in Anderson, Indiana, before coming to Headquarters as a candidate for Congo. He was tiny. His baggage was tinier. He arrived with one small case, little larger than an attache case in size. But he had a tremendous devotion to Christ and a spirit of sacrifice like the Mission founder, C. T. Studd. Nothing was too much trouble for Bill in those candidate days. And he was always writing poetry. Here are some of his lines:

"*My Choice*"

I want my breakfast served at "Eight"
With ham and eggs upon the plate.
A well-broiled steak I'll eat at "One",
And dine again when day is done.

I want an ultra-modern home,
And in each room a telephone;
Soft carpets, too, upon the floors,
And pretty drapes to grace the doors.

A cosy place of lovely things,
Like easy chairs with inner springs;
And then I'll get a small T.V.—
Of course, I'm careful what I see.

25

I want my wardrobe, too, to be
Of neatest, finest quality,
With latest style in suit and vest.
Why shouldn't Christians have the best?

But then the Master I can hear,
In no uncertain voice, so clear,
"I bid you come and follow Me,
The lowly Man of Galilee.

"Birds of the air have made their nest,
And foxes in their holes find rest;
But I can offer you no bed;
No place have I to lay My head."

In shame I hung my head and cried.
How could I spurn the Crucified?
Could I forget the way He went,
The sleepless nights in prayer He spent?

For forty days without a bite,
Alone He fasted day and night;
Despised, rejected—on He went,
And did not stop till veil He rent.

A Man of Sorrows and of grief,
No earthly friend to bring relief—
"Smitten of God," the prophet said—
Mocked, beaten, bruised, His blood ran red.

If He be God and died for me,
No sacrifice too great can be
For me, a mortal man, to make;
I'll do it all for Jesus' sake.

Yes, I will tread the path He trod,
No other way will please my God;
So henceforth, this my choice shall be,
My choice for all eternity.

Little did we know, as we said goodbye to Bill in 1959, that a few years later, the first line of that last verse would become true as he was martyred for Christ by merciless Simbas in the Congo rebellion. He was a gentleman to the last. Two Catholic nuns who saw him shortly before the end said, "He had the face of an angel."

Strange that we had a small share in helping to prepare a Scottish school teacher, Jim Rodger, who trained with us in Glasgow, and Bill McChesney of Phoenix, both of whom laid down their lives in that Congo holocaust. And what an awesome responsibility to be involved in the preparation of today's young people. "Lord! Keep us at the foot of the Cross so that Thy resurrection life may flow through and minister to the needs of these whom You are calling to service."

So we saw Bill and a number of other North American candidates off to the field between 1957 and 1960. This responsibility came to an end and then, with our tasks taken over by others, we were invited by W.E.C. Australia to take charge of the rapidly developing Missionary Training College in Launceston, Tasmania.

"Tasmania?" we thought. "What on earth will it be like, away at the bottom of the world?" "Why, we'll have the nearest W.E.C. centre to the South Pole, if that is any distinction."

Tasmania is only dimly remembered by most Britishers from their school study of British Commonwealth geography. To Americans it is virtually unknown.

"Tasmania?" one Philadelphian sales-clerk asked us. "Do the natives have houses down there?"

What was the will of God in this? Certainly circumstances pointed in the direction of Australia.

27

There was no immediate likelihood of the North American school commencing. There was no pressing involvement in the North American home end. An urgent need existed in Australia, and a unanimous invitation had come from the Australian staff for us to help them. Out in the woods, and alone with God, the cry went up, "What are You saying in this, Lord?" And quietly, but with a glow of assurance came the thought—

"What has been your commission in W.E.C. all along?"

"To do as occasion serves. Fit in to the need of the fellowship."

"Well, is this not such an occasion?"

"But Lord, it means severing a second set of friendships. And it means uprooting the children from their education."

"My will is best."

"All right, Lord."

Some time after posting a letter indicating our willingness to go to Australia, a cable arrived one Monday from Sydney:

"IMPERATIVE DINNENS ARRIVE IN ONE WEEK".

The American staff agreed to our release and then followed five days of packing, freighting, giving away or storing our bits and pieces. However, we met the deadline, leaving Philadelphia the following Friday, stopping overnight in Los Angeles at the W.E.C. Headquarters and flying out on Saturday for Sydney.

We could not go to church on Sunday, May 22nd, 1960. There was no such day for us because we crossed the International Date Line, arriving on Monday morning to be met by Arthur Davidson, secretary of W.E.C. in Australia.

We came from eighty-five degrees warmth to

thirty-five degrees cold (at nights) with no central heating. Misery!

Night was now day. Early summer was now early winter. Our daughter, Ruth, having changed from pennies and shillings in the U.K. to dollars and cents in U.S.A., found herself doing sums in pennies and shillings again, only to be told that soon the Australian currency would be converted to dollars and cents. Poor kid, her mathematics have never been the best. "I have learned in whatsoever state I am therewith to be content." Ours was to be the State of Tasmania, so we had to face the adjustment and learn speedily.

3

Building

WE arrived either on or near the shortest day of the year, and that meant the longest night. Truly it was the long night of our experience.

Before leaving the U.S.A. someone had been led to say that days of darkness were ahead of us, but that there would be added responsibility and increased fruitfulness in the final outcome.

As we came to grips with the local situation at the Missionary Training College at St. Leonards, near Launceston, Tasmania, we had the feeling of entering a dark tunnel.

The College had fifty students from Australia and New Zealand preparing for missionary service. Due to problems and mistakes which are best left untold, we found the College divided over doctrine, and largely bereft of the support of the Christian public. In this situation we sought to steer a delicate course of rehabilitation and re-orientation, but we were to a large extent unsuccessful. A few weeks after we arrived, the majority of the students and all the staff left to commence a new independent college with a distinct doctrinal emphasis, and we were left with sixteen students determined to follow in the W.E.C. tradition.

The forty-five acre property had a small farm, and we two city slickers found ourselves also loaded with eight cows, half-a-dozen pigs, a horse and a dog. Fortunately the W.E.C. Headquarters in Brisbane came to our rescue and sent staff worker Clem Smoker who knew enough about farming to keep us going. Later we had the help, for a time, of Ken Williams on furlough from Indonesia and Edna Parish from India.

Looking back, what a "scratch" crew we were! Clem with the cows, Marie on catering plus the organising of women's and men's practical duties, myself buried in the study, grappling with the problem of keeping a full Bible School curriculum in action.

The very extremity of the situation forced us into totally new methods. When, some weeks previously, this eventuality had been envisaged, the prayer had been, "Lord, reveal a system of Bible study that will be satisfying to the students and at the same time keep me from being bogged down in a spoon-feeding lecture routine."

The Lord gave a plan, and to this day we have used our guided personal search system which has proved its worth as a satisfying method of assimilating Scriptural truth, through keeping the student personally involved in direct investigation of the Word.

What a grand bunch of students it was who withstood the shock-wave of this transition to a new staff, a new system, a new tempo, and a new missionary outlook! The Scotlands—Tom, an ex-Air Force pilot and civil engineer and his wife, Laurel, now in charge of the production of the free Gospel news-sheet *SOON* in Sydney; the Willises, now leaders of the W.E.C. Youth Crusade in New South Wales, from whose ranks dozens of young people have moved into training; young banker Moorhouse who went to Thailand; diesel engine driver Ivan Ross who has been pioneering in Brazil; motor mechanic Peter Belchamber now a youth worker in Ivory Coast; Jim Sterrey now a pioneer in West Irian with the Asia Pacific Christian Mission, and others of similar calibre—Dave Enright in Sumatra, Alan King in Venezuela.

31

But how could this "shoe-string" outfit survive? No finance was coming in; there were hardly any outlets for student activity; public meetings were poorly attended; young people were discouraged from applying. "Lord, where do we go from here?" Instantly, as if, movie-projector fashion, it had been switched on to the screen of my mind, there stood one word, indelibly printed—**Resurrection.**

With the Scots temperament coming to the surface, the reply was, "Lord, as far as I can see we ought to pack up, but if by any chance you *do* mean **Resurrection** we need an instant shot in the arm of about two hundred dollars, and I trust you for $1,000 by the time the executive meets to decide the future of the College."

Within a week we had almost that first amount in small gifts from unexpected sources—but not a cent more for weeks on end, till the very day of the executive meeting in Sydney when the long term policy for the College had to be finalised. One hour before leaving, a letter arrived in the mail from a Launceston solicitor. It read:

"Mr. . . . died on the 15th instant, and under his Will, left the sum of $1,000 to your trust, to be used in Tasmania for any purpose that the governing authorities of the College think fit."

We stayed! And as we stayed, out of sheer obedience, we began to emerge from the tunnel.

The student intake the following year was small—only six—but God's hand was in this because we saw Him beginning to provide the permanent staff. Of these six, three are now members of the College staff.

Exactly a year after arriving in Tasmania, a new challenge of faith had to be met. As Principal I was expected to attend W.E.C.'s first International Leaders' Conference in Britain in May 1961. Travelling expenses were a personal responsibility. We had to trust the Lord that this extra cost would be met by gifts that would not otherwise have gone to the fields—a tricky assignment! But God, of course, was faithful and, little by little, all that was needed for the basic air fare came in, from different and some surprising donors in many parts of the world.

The plan was to travel via New Zealand, spending a week there for meetings in view of the interest in the College among young people.

A few days before leaving, a cable arrived: "CAN YOU TAKE EXTRA MEETING CHRIST-CHURCH". This would involve an extra return air fare Auckland-Christchurch costing sixty dollars; at that time I did not have twenty-five cents over and above the basic fare! "What do I do, Lord?" There was peace—and faith—to cable back: "ACCEPT CHRISTCHURCH MEETING".

The next morning a local business man was awakened early with the distinct impression that he had to send sixty dollars to me immediately. How encouraged he was to hear later that this met the need exactly!

A few days later I took this small and uneventful meeting in a chilly hall in fog-bound Christchurch. Next morning a lad drifted over to the car where I sat, ready to be taken to the airport.

"Mr. Dinnen, God has called me to be a missionary and I feel I should train at the W.E.C. College in Tasmania."

It was hard to imagine that this young man could be missionary material. Squat and overweight, with unruly hair and diffident, shy manner; what could God make of this?

"What do you do for a living?"

"I'm a glass blower."

"A glass blower! And what were you doing before that?"

"I was a cream taster in a butter factory."

"And you feel you should be a missionary?"

"Well . . . yes."

"Pray about it and if you still feel certain in a month's time, write to us and we'll take it from there."

A little wet blanket treatment won't do you any harm, I thought to myself. If you are real, you will press through.

When I returned, there was his application in neat handwriting, the words spelled correctly. We sent forms, and these, too, were later returned completed carefully and accurately. There was really no adequate reason for turning him down.

Maurice Charman came. Young—yes. Inexperienced—yes. Immature—yes. (He actually managed to board the wrong plane in Melbourne en route to Tasmania and would have ended up 1,000 miles from his correct destination but for a sympathetic airline pilot who wheeled the plane back to the terminal building and let him off.) But he was open, ready and willing for all that God had to show him.

We jump ahead for a moment to 1969 and the W.E.C. Annual Meeting in Sydney where, convicted and humiliated, I sat enthralled to hear the same Maurice give his testimony of five years' service in Taiwan.

". . . and my final assignment before leaving the field for furlough was a strange one. I was asked by a group of Chinese nuclear physicists if I would lead them in a series of Bible Studies.

" 'In English?' I asked.

" 'No, in Chinese, please.'

" 'Well, what book will we study?'

" 'We are most interested in the future of Israel. We want to study Zechariah,' they said."

Here, then, was Maurice Charman, the glass blower, the cream taster, teaching Chinese nuclear physicists the book of Zechariah in Chinese. What miracles of grace can be accomplished when the heart is obedient!

That 1961 trip to the W.E.C. Kilcreggan Conference was not without other adventures and encouragements.

When finalising plans for my return via Holland, Thailand and Indonesia, I had been holding before the Lord the question of how much time to spend in Holland with Brother Andrew, "God's Smuggler", who had trained with us in our British W.E.C. College. I knew he had much to share, so much that could not safely be written or published at that time.

Should I spend just one day with him, or remain overnight? I had the sense, in my spirit, that overnight was right. And true enough, Andrew kept me up well after midnight sharing his amazing experiences. He had just returned from East Germany after over-staying the expiry date of his visa, so he had asked the Lord to blind the eyes of the two inspectors when he came out. Prayer was answered and there we were rejoicing together over the Lord's goodness.

Next morning we drove to the airport to find the place in a turmoil. The plane I would have been on had I left the night before, had crashed at Cairo and half the occupants had been killed.

So it was home again, after stops in Thailand and Indonesia, to a most affectionate welcome from wife and family who, because of a mail-strike, had failed to receive word of my flight plans and had thought for several days that I had been on the crashed plane. It is good to know you are wanted!

4

Developing

THE development of the College programme in the early sixties would have been completely impossible apart from the loyal, devoted team which the Lord called and led into fellowship with us during that time.

Evan Davies, now vice-principal, was born of W.E.C. missionary parents in Congo and grew up in the W.E.C. Missionary Children's Home in Arbroath, Scotland. He had emigrated to New Zealand when his father, Ivor, was appointed General Secretary for W.E.C. in that country. With such a background his W.E.C. "outlook" was truly assured. Jenny Grocke, who became Jenny Davies, was every inch a Crusader, too. She had been brought to the Lord through the evangelistic ministry of her uncle, Murray Wilkes, member of W.E.C. in Adelaide. Another convert of Murray's was a slightly-built young lass called Valda Williams. Medical considerations hindered her from applying for overseas service after training but, once accepted into the Crusade, she returned to take up the very strategic role of college secretary and treasurer, a task which she has carried with devotion and diligence in spite of physical limitations.

Reviewing the past eight years during which we five have worked together we can truly say that the free flow of open fellowship that has existed between us has been one of the highlights of our spiritual pilgrimage.

And this glorious by-product of the faith-and-obedience life has come about not because we are specially gifted, longsuffering, gracious people, but simply because we have recognised the fundamental lesson that fellowship can only be maintained at the foot of the Cross; that is, with real honesty that calls sin sin, and with a two-way exercise of brokenness and forgiveness, which keeps short accounts between one another.

Others have helped for a time in various capacities and their contributions have been valuable and significant: Lloyd and Jean Timms on the small College farm of forty acres; Bruce and Annette Rattray who took over from them while awaiting their visas to Borneo; Graham and Marjorie Bee who "inherited" the farm from Bruce and Annette; Margaret Hewitt on catering and teaching; Ivan Bowden, a school-teacher from Queensland who gave years of magnificent teaching and married Luba Koznedelev who supervised the kitchen for a time.

As leaders of this team, carrying the double responsibility of guiding staff and training students, we knew that the only hope of success lay in establishing the work firmly and squarely on sound spiritual principles.

Looking back we can see how the Lord started to prepare us for this, long years before we had any thought of coming to Tasmania.

Marie and I had both drunk deeply at the fountain of Norman Grubb's ministry. He had been responsible, under God, for the development of W.E.C. after the death of C. T. Studd, but he was far more than a mission administrator. The impact of his teaching ministry has been felt all over the English-speaking world.

The first time I heard him was just after completing

a high school teacher's course. It was a shattering experience for a puffed-up young graduate.

"We're not concerned about degrees," he said, and then with that curious side-jerk of his head which we came to recognise as the harbinger of some mischievous dig . . . "Men *die* by degrees." And then he went on to expound true discipleship.

Later we came to know this great missionary statesman both through his books and spoken messages, and also, during our two-and-a-half year stay in the Philadelphia headquarters, when we lived only a few steps along the corridor from his apartments.

He was our Winston Churchill in the spiritual realm. We loved him for his deep ministry in the things of God and that unique charisma whereby he was able to convey to the youngest of workers that he believed in them, respected them, and trusted them implicitly. He had an infinite resource of patience and forbearance that mystically transmitted the sense that he really wanted our fellowship, and we knew that we could go to him at any time with any matter, confident that he would apply himself just as totally to our five cents' worth of problem as to his own.

Furthermore, he lived the life of faith and personal sacrifice before us. He consistently poured large personal gifts received on preaching tours into Mission projects. When travelling with him one could never get the better of him in paying for petrol or meals. Generous American friends often sent boxes of clothes to him. On one occasion some particularly fine quality suits and ties came from the widow of a recently deceased business man who was Norman's very height and build. But he insisted on the other junior workers looking through these and taking what they wanted before he had a turn—and this was not because he already had more than enough. His wardrobe contained the barest minimum. He really lived Christ.

So the principles that had been lived before our eyes and now burned in our hearts were the total sufficiency of Christ and, through surrender and faith, realised union with Him. Two other essentials of discipleship had "rubbed off" on us through our long association with Weccers over the years, particularly Fran and Elsie Rowbotham—constructive fellowship and creative faith.

The story of how the first two principles were applied comes in Chapter Five. At this point, for the sake of continuity in the school development story, we deal with the latter two.

As a staff, we knew we had to be completely one with the students and we realised that this was impossible without openness and sharing on as many levels as practicable.

So we sought to identify with them in various activities. Several mornings a week we would study a New Testament epistle together, expounding thoroughly but also encouraging student participation through questions, inviting opinions, or giving opportunity to testify in line with the point under discussion.

We shared nearly every meal with them in the college dining room. We joined in manual tasks on the property when our programme permitted. With forty-five acres and a small farm there was a fair amount of this, and each student worked outside for two afternoons a week. Our staff apartments were right on campus, and we were available for fellowship and counselling when needed. We established a regular counselling system so that every student had periodic sessions with a staff member so that each knew how we felt regarding progress.

Of course, there were formal lectures and classes,

but the dominant note in the College atmosphere was the learning and application of spiritual principles rather than the assimilation of abstract knowledge and the associated drive for mere academic distinction.

Recollecting college days, a former student, now a staff member of another Bible Institute, wrote:

"A memorable incident occurred during one Saturday morning practical session. A mind not praising the Lord is ground for the enemy. Just as I was wishing I was anywhere but here, getting water in my boots, a staff member came out in his old attire and joined me in the task. Somehow this seemed to change my attitude and I finished the morning rejoicing. It made all the difference to other practical sessions I engaged in after that. I was grateful that sometimes staff found time to join us in practical aspects of the work even though their time usually was fully taken up."

Another graduate writes:

"College years were some of the best years of my life, though some of the hardest. So much could be said, but to me the most outstanding feature of college was the family atmosphere. We all had a feeling of 'belonging'. Right from the beginning I was part of this family and we belonged to one another. It was hard to leave after Graduation, but that sense of belonging to a family rather than an organisation still exists today as I prepare to leave soon for the field."

As regards creative faith, we have purposely kept the rate of student fees at seventy per cent of what is actually needed to keep the college solvent. (Staff, of course, receive no remuneration from College funds but trust the Lord independently for His supply. How can we teach faith to students unless we are exercising it ourselves?)

40

We therefore have a continuing situation in which as a college fellowship we must trust the Lord for the remaining thirty per cent of what is needed. We instituted a session of prayer—or rather of faith—one afternoon every two weeks when we are quite open with the students about material needs and spiritual objectives, so that, in oneness of fellowship and in creative faith, we can express ourselves positively and expectantly before the Lord on every issue.

One former student wrote to us recently from her mission field:

"We are facing a brick-wall situation here at the moment. How we thank God for the memory of those days in College when we prayed through, and saw God's power released in direct response to creative faith."

At one stage there had been a particularly fine spell of growth on the College farm. Bruce Rattray said:

"We could use two more cows, the feed is so good."

"Yes, it would be nice if we had two more cows," I replied.

But somehow we failed to take direct action by way of positive faith until time came round for one of our afternoons of prayer. Again Bruce spoke to us.

"We really must trust the Lord for these two cows."

That afternoon we shared the position with the students and in prayer we said, "We know this seems a bit odd, Lord, but we are asking and receiving from you two more cows."

The prayer time finished about 4.30 p.m. Just after 5 p.m. a Christian couple who own a dairy farm fifty miles away drove in.

"Stewart, we are reducing our herd and we have the strangest urge that you ought to be getting two of our best cows. Is this right? Are we doing the right thing?"

41

The impact of the news, shared with the students at the evening meal, was electric!

On another occasion we had observed, on going through our accounts, how much had been spent on printing notices for meetings, students' missions, and so on. It came home to us that the sensible answer to this problem was to have our own print shop.

We had nothing for this in our bank account and we knew of no suitable machine available for sale in Tasmania. However, we took it to the fellowship in one afternoon of prayer and there was a spontaneous rise amongst students and staff that this was a God-given target for creative faith. So we *told* the Lord we were expecting Him to give us this machine. It had to be a simple one, not too large, not necessarily new, but adequate for the elementary work we envisaged.

The next day in the mail we received a letter from a young man in Melbourne who had been a student with us. In it he said:

"I just sense that I have to get this cheque off to you today. I don't know why, but the Lord has burdened me to send you this amount of $400 to be used FOR ANY PROJECT YOU HAVE IN MIND AT THE MOMENT."

The next day the local paper carried an advertisement for a small second-hand printing machine—the very size we wanted—plus a stapler and a cutter. These were the three essential pieces of equipment for our new printshop. The owner was willing to sell the lot for $230 but, being a Scot, I offered him $200—and he took it!

Imagine the students' reaction when our truck drove in, five days after the prayer of creative faith, with the printing machine on board!

The story does not end there because, shortly after, the parents of one of our students from Western

Australia came East for a vacation and decided to spend two weeks with us at the College. The father turned out to be a printer and when I showed him our machine lying dismantled in the tiny room that was to become our printshop, he said:

"Mr. Dinnen, I know every nut and bolt on this model. I used to work one of these. I'll be delighted to set it up for you, and train two of the students so that you can keep it going when I leave."

That machine has hardly had an idle day since!

Recollecting his early training in creative faith, an ex-student wrote:

"One lesson that I learnt at the very beginning was of implicit trust in the Lord in every realm, spiritual, material and physical. One vivid experience came in my second year when I was taken to hospital for an operation. I had previously seen a specialist and he had decided that, though there was not much evidence, I should have an exploratory operation for possible cancer. I had been going through a particularly hard emotional and spiritual situation at college and this was the Lord's way of teaching me. I accepted this as from Him, and when I did, His peace just flooded me. The operation proved that the tentative diagnosis was not correct but that I had another condition that needed treatment.

"After a week I was out of hospital and back at college. I was relying on the Lord for college fees and daily needs, so was a bit concerned about the cost of the operation (thirteen dollars fifty) and the week in hospital (forty-four dollars). This, of course, was not much on a working man's wage but, to me, waiting for the Lord's deliverance for fees, it was quite a sum. I had not a cent. Could He now meet this need?

"A week or two passed in which I received a few more reminders till the final notice came. My faith started to quiver a little. I went before the Lord, opened my Bible and found the old promises concerning needs and how He would meet them.

"I said, 'Lord, I simply receive your supply right now,' and I began to praise Him for it, even though I did not have it in the physical realm. Once I thanked Him, I felt a wonderful sense of His assurance and peace.

"As the day progressed, I received in the mail $10. Then a College student, not knowing my needs, came up to me and said, 'I tithe what the Lord sends in for me, and I believe He wants you to have this tithe.' It was $3.50. So the Specialist's fee was covered. No one knew of the hospital bill, but, about two hours later, another person handed me a cheque, saying that the Lord had guided him to give it to me. The cheque was for $44. To the cent the Lord was faithful. From this and countless other experiences, I know the Lord is well able to handle all my needs."

Our practical emphasis whereby students work two afternoons a week on the property not only results in their learning new skills, but also keeps our operating costs low. Expensive tradesmen's bills are kept to a minimum and new developments can be undertaken for the cost of materials only. Of course, student help alone would be insufficient, but one of God's miracles has been to bring Christian businessmen and tradesmen alongside us, using their skills and resources in helping to develop the property. Their testimony is that the fellowship and joy they receive out of doing this for the Lord far outweighs their own loss of time—and energy!

On several occasions a team of men, containing at least one carpenter and one bricklayer, from a church sixty-five miles away have given a whole Saturday, leaving home in the early morning and working right through the daylight hours erecting new buildings. In one such project the framework for two offices, three bedrooms, living room and bathroom were erected in twelve hours.

Recently another Christian builder, assisted by a team of students, erected the steel frame (prefabricated) for a new workshop—covering nearly 3,500 square feet—in ninety minutes flat.

On one occasion, during the College vacation, we "bit off more than we could chew". We had decided to re-floor the women's dormitories, where it was far too easy for the girls to put their shoe heels in the large spaces between the eighty-year old wooden planks. All went well in the ripping-up stage, but in the re-flooring we struck some complications that needed the know-how of a professional carpenter. In our supper-time prayer session that night we said, "Lord, we can't go any further; please send us a carpenter tomorrow."

Next morning a local Christian carpenter, Lubberd Bosveld, who at that time knew little about us, phoned and said:

"The materials for the job I'm working on haven't arrived. Could you use a carpenter today?"

On another occasion we were up almost to roof level, again in vacation time, and none of us knew how to tie in the new brick wall to the roof. Furthermore, our transport situation was aggravated by one of our trucks breaking down. That night we said:

"Lord, we've got two problems. We don't know how to tie this brick wall into the roof properly, and we've got a Dodge that won't budge. Please do something."

Next day I had a phone call from seventy-five miles away:

"Stewart Dinnen? I hear from someone who visited the College yesterday that you're having prob-

45

lems trying to finish a new extension. Can you use me for three days?"

Could we use him? Bob was not merely a brick-layer, but a builder of wide experience able to solve all our problems. Furthermore, without any knowledge of our transport problem, he brought along his son who was a final year apprentice motor mechanic!

Often the Lord has called into training young men whose particular skills have been exactly suited to the type of work in which we were involved during their stay—a joiner (Ron Webb) when we needed window frames for the new lecture hall; a Volkswagen mechanic (Peter Belchamber) when we had a Volkswagen Kombi; Evan Davies, experienced in book room management, who came on the staff when our literature programme was developing; Jim Ross, concrete worker, when we needed a new septic tank.

And our testimony is that, while these skills were extremely valuable, these men did not lose out on their necessary study time. We have consistently taken the stand that practical projects are subservient to the training and evangelistic programme.

5

Training

THE thrust of our teaching has been to help the
student to realise his total human inadequacy, and
then to see and appropriate Christ's complete sufficiency
ministered to him in the power of the Holy Spirit.

The process can be painful in the initial stages and
many testify that the first year is a year of conviction,
a year of acute dealings, as the Holy Spirit reveals self
in all its ugly forms. Then the second year is usually a
time of grounding in the things of the Spirit, and the
developing of faith.

It is not easy to stand on the touchline and watch
the process go on, but it would be fatal for us to hinder
what God is doing. We simply encourage everyone to
be, above all else, honest before God, and to accept
whatever He is seeking to say through the Word and
through circumstances.

One girl, a former school teacher and now a valued
missionary making a vital contribution to the conversion of the heathen in India, came to my office one day.

"Mr. Dinnen, I've come to a realisation that I don't
think I've got what it takes to get through this course."

"Well, that's just fine!"

"But Mr. Dinnen" (in crestfallen tones), "I thought
you'd be able to give me some encouragement. Instead
of that . . ."

"No. I'm not here to give you encouragement. I
just want you to face reality."

"I just feel I'm so unqualified."

47

"Wonderful. That's exactly the place you have to reach before God can trust you with the power of His Spirit."

"Oh!"

"Can't you see that your very first qualification is to realise that you are totally unqualified. Only then can God get the glory. 'Blessed are the poor in spirit: for their's is the kingdom of heaven.'"

She saw it!

Towards the end of training she came again. This time she was beaming.

"Mr. Dinnen, I'm clear about my call. God has clearly spoken to me."

"Oh, yes."

"You don't seem very keen to hear, Mr. Dinnen."

"Well, I am in one way, but frankly something else needs to happen first."

"What's that?"

"You yourself have said how some days you are up in 'the glory' and other days really depressed."

"Yes, I've never really licked that problem yet."

"You'll have to be steady on the field."

"I know."

"Why not take by faith the promise, 'Jesus Christ the same yesterday, and to day, and for ever'?"

"I see."

"Let's pray then."

And she settled down to a steady purposeful walk with the Lord.

Another student writes:

"W.E.C. is a faith mission. As a new student in college I was quite self-sufficient and knew nothing of having to trust God to supply my needs. As other students joyfully testified to God's supply I longed that He would do this for me too. But at the time I had plenty of money to see me through. Yet I longed that

The Dinnen Family

College Staff 1970

| Ivan Bowden | Luba Bowden | Margt. Hewitt | Marj Bee | Graham Bee |
| Val Williams | Marie Dinnen | Stewart Dinnen | Jenny Davies | Evan Davies |

WHERE DO THEY GO?

We have included this photograph, taken in 1964, in order to show something of the strategy of the Spirit in preparing and directing lives into the purpose of God.

Beside the names are listed the fields to which graduates went after training. The few with an asterisk are in secular work.

Front Row left to right: Avrille Campbell (nee Kent), Ghana; Pam Rowlands, Brazil; Alison Shadbolt (nee Gordon), India; Mattie Gardiner,★ Scotland; Glenys Osborne (nee Baigent), Senegal; Lois Jensen,★ Queensland; Jan Taylor, Thailand; Grace Moorhouse, Chad; Rhonda Sallaway, Japan.

Second Row left to right: Deidre Cornish, India (now glorified); Ivan Bowden, Val Williams, Stewart and Marie Dinnen, M.T.C. Staff; Bruce and Annette Rattray, M.T.C. Staff, now Borneo; Ken Watson, Venezuela.

Third Row left to right: Don Whisson,★ West Australia, Ian Crowe, Ivory Coast; Margot Whisson,★ West Australia; Carol Cardinal, "Soon", Sydney; Joan Mundy, Brazil; Sue Sutherland★ (nee Lowther), New Zealand; Diane Dick (nee Wilkinson), Chad; Joy Watson (nee Walkden), Venezuela; Lorraine Lymburn, Baptist Ministry; Jan Thomas, Congo; Joan Clarke, Teen Challenge, Auckland; Lyn Salisbury (nee Fleming), Open Air Campaigners, Christchurch; Ian Lymburn, Baptist Ministry, South Australia; Alan Shadbolt, India.

Back Row left to right: Ian Cook, Thailand; James Gardiner,★ Scotland; John McInnes,★ Brisbane; Trevor Woodland,★ New South Wales; Don Dick, Chad; David Townshend, Brazil; Chas. Osborne, Senegal; Peter Horrell, Colombia; Peter Scrimgeour, Brazil; James Ross, Solomon Islands.

Missionary Training College, Tasmania

The Study Room

The Library

God would take it, so that I could depend on Him alone. Faith needs to be developed and sometimes we trust God for little things before we have confidence to trust Him for bigger things. This is what I learned during my first four terms. God was preparing me gradually.

"My fifth term arrived and I still had sufficient funds. But God said, 'Now it's time to launch out and trust Me.' Even after all that the Lord had revealed of the life of faith I still had reservations and my conservative reasoning rebelled. But my heart said, 'Yes, Lord.' This was the beginning of a new and thrilling experience of being dependent on God. Several days after I had given the remainder of my money to the Lord He did a lovely thing for me. As I returned to my dormitory one night, there, under my clock, was a one dollar note. It was a token of God's love to me and an assurance that He would supply my needs.

"This was lovely, but faith is strengthened through stretching. As the term concluded God wonderfully supplied my fees, but then I needed my fare home for Christmas. God allowed me to wait right up till the night before I was due to leave before my fare came. I still had no money for food on the two days' journey home. As I packed my last few things on the departure day I knew God would not let me down. And He didn't. Picking up my Bible to put in my case, I opened it and there in the cover was a two dollar bill, just for this need.

"The story was similar in my last term—God stretching, then wonderfully delivering. When one has nothing, every little thing that God gives reflects His love and goodness and gives one a greater love and appreciation for our Heavenly Father."

One young man wrote:

"Perhaps the most important lesson the Lord

began to teach me in college was, 'In everything give thanks.' I learned to look behind difficult circumstances and see a loving God who was only bringing pressure on me to prove me and draw me closer to Himself. One divine formula was mentioned many times in college—'Pressure produces patience and patience maturity and maturity hope' (Rom. 5: 3, 4).

"God's way of bringing pressure to bear on me was through physical weakness. The Lord gave me about five weeks of good health; the rest was struggle. Things I used to be able to do in my own strength became impossible. Study hours were reduced, assignments and duties were harder to perform, and overseas service looked unlikely. It just seemed that there was too much pressure. All that I had hoped for appeared to fade. Then when life was a real strain God revealed Himself in a wonderful way. I suddenly re-discovered who God really was—my strength, joy, peace, confidence, everything. He became my joy—not circumstances, health or anything else. I found that the verse 'My grace is sufficient for thee' was in the present tense. It was for me—now.

"It seemed that God was constantly allowing me to get into situations where my reserves were inadequate that I might draw from His limitless resources. In coming to an end of myself I found God to be all that He has promised to be. It was only pressure that brought me into a wealthy place of a new love for God and simple dependence on Him.

"In fact, it is not the battles and victories that one remembers most from college so much as the simple joy of coming to know the Lord in a deeper and fuller way."

Another student battled over the issue of surrender and sacrifice. Before training he had been an engineer with QANTAS, the Australian airline, and with his private pilot's licence and progress towards his commercial rating, he "had it made" if he stayed with the Company. But God called him to M.T.C. and to W.E.C.

"I well remember", he said in testimony once, "doing an afternoon of practical work. It happened to be in the garden, digging carrots out of Tasmanian mud. The airport is close by and I watched the jets as they flew over. Satan said, 'Alan, you could be flying one of those for a big wage, instead of digging carrots for nothing.'"

But time passed and, in yieldedness to Christ, he too found his way to India from where he wrote recently:

"We have had much opportunity for ministry among students in colleges, hostels, Christian fellowships, and so on. We praise Him for the way He has blessed and owned this from the very beginning. We leave soon to speak at an Easter Convention. Not since college days have I known the Spirit of God to be so real and active in our midst."

Better brimful of blessings in Bombay than bankrupt in Boeings!

Very often the Lord, in the process of dealing with self, deals with self's possessions. Of all people who knew this dealing with riches, one who truly faced it to the depths was a girl called just that—RICHES!

It was in 1963 when she was a student that our faith battle raged round the construction of the new lecture hall. For some time we knew the inevitable must be faced because our largest room was totally inadequate for this purpose. Days of prayer, discussion, proposal and counter-proposal passed, without any clear assurance.

Then, as Marie and I walked around the main building one day, it came to us like a bolt of lightning.

51

We suddenly realised that the old driveway round the original front was no longer necessary because the 'back' had become the 'front' with the erection of a main door, foyer and dining hall.

"Let's build out over the old driveway where it is quiet, away from visiting vehicles, and there's a beautiful view down the valley to the river."

Here was the spot, secluded from public gaze, yet next to a large hallway which could become the library. It all clicked into place—as things do when the pattern is from the Lord. Other staff members agreed. A Christian bricklayer was contacted; plans were drawn up and passed; and our friend Reg Price, a steel fabricator in Hobart, 120 miles away, got busy with his welding apparatus making the steel trusses.

Although the roofing trusses were delivered to us as a gift (for which we were tremendously grateful), we still needed money for bricks, concrete, etc. We brought the matter before the Lord and our hearts came to a place of rest.

One day Doreen Riches, who had been a school teacher, came to my office. Shyly sharing how God had dealt with her over possessions, she said she would like to leave an envelope to help towards the cost of the lecture hall.

I was very pleased to see Doreen's surrender to the Lord, for its own sake, and rather suspected that there would be fifty dollars or maybe a one hundred dollar cheque in the envelope. Imagine the reaction to find that it was for $1,300!

She had emptied her bank book to help pay for the lecture hall. Was it right to take it? Was this just a momentary youthful impulse? I talked with her and queried her motives, but found her quite clear, and very determined. Besides, how could the Principal seriously question something like this, when God had led him a similar way in training days?

But you can't beat God at giving! The Lord took Doreen to France and then to Ivory Coast, where she had a quiet, steady witness during her first term. On furlough five years later she re-visited the College for a four day stay, a dedicated Crusader who endeared herself to the hearts of the women students particularly.

In an inquisitive mood I asked her privately,

"Doreen, since you're leaving next month for Ivory Coast again, may I ask how you stand for your finance?"

She did not want to tell me at first, but I insisted.

"Well, I have quite a bit towards my return fare, but I still need three hundred dollars towards that, and several hundreds more for equipment for the Missionary Children's School we will be starting."

I said nothing, but next day during our afternoon of prayer I suggested that as a fellowship we should be standing in faith for the supply of Doreen's needs.

Over the succeeding forty-eight hours God did a wonderful thing in our midst. Not from any wealthy outside source, but from the students themselves, little bits started to arrive at the office earmarked for Doreen. When she left next day, we were able to give her a cheque for over $500.

It was then that the memory of her gift came flooding back, and after she had gone, I was able to use this as an illustration of the Lord's ways with us.

Very often students commence the course without having all the two years' fees saved beforehand. Is it wrong for us to accept them in such circumstances? Of course not! They have to learn to trust the Lord and, provided they have not been foolish with what they have earned before training, we can believe the Lord for His supply.

We do have a rule, however, that no one can commence a new term until the previous one is completely paid up.

We well remember reaching the end of one term and several had still to clear their obligations with the office. The matter had been earnestly held before the Lord.

In the midst of our festivities—the last night of term is usually a hilarious fun-and-games night, followed by a testimony time—I was called out to the phone. A Christian business man wanted to make a donation, and felt he wanted to let me know THAT NIGHT! The amount was just what was needed to clear the fees.

If there was joy in the festivities there was joy unspeakable when I made the announcement later!

Avrille Campbell (née Kent) now in Ghana writes:

"After two terms in M.T.C. I decided to entrust my bank balance to the Lord. I wanted to prove that God could provide my needs just as He did for others. This included fees for the term. On the last Saturday of term I still needed fourteen dollars. In my heart I had determined not to go home until that debt was paid. It was Conference Day and Graduation for some students. I wondered if the Lord would send something through the mail. Not a bean. In the afternoon as I was washing dishes a staff member (Val) approached me with a letter in her hand. It had been mixed up with the staff mail. For some reason my father had sent me ten dollars. It had never happened before! But I was still four dollars short. However, faith rose in my heart because if the Lord could provide ten, He could also provide four. Later in the day a Christian brother told me he had wanted to see me last month but had missed out. With that, he pressed four dollars into my hand. (The Lord is still as faithful here in Ghana, too!)"

So it has been intensely fascinating to see this

younger generation of Abrahams grasp the potential of bold creative faith and prove it dynamic in their own particular spheres, firstly on the personal elementary "tooth paste" level and then right on into field and home end projects that are having international ramifications. A typical example of this is the development under the leadership of graduates Tom and Laurel Scotland of the *SOON* free Gospel News-sheet programme for South East Asia. Inspired by the vision of Secretary Arthur Davidson, they have advanced from a shoestring one-room short-staffed beginning, and have boldly proved God in provision of more and more equipment and the raising up of dozens of *SOON* wrapping-and-mailing groups all over Australia and New Zealand. Today thousands upon thousands of copies of this Gospel newspaper are read all over the South Pacific area and hundreds are writing in, requesting advice on becoming Christians, and enrolling for simple Bible correspondence courses.

The project literally commenced with twenty-five cents—their total assets at the start. Today five full-time workers are committed to this programme and each issue involves the expenditure of hundreds of dollars.

A training programme that inculcates living principles means that instead of "adding" we are "multiplying"; the disciples become reproducers.

6

Spreading

IT would be poor training for work with the World-wide Evangelization Crusade if there was little emphasis on evangelism. Fortunately the College location offers an excellent opportunity both for local outreach in the city and surroundings of Launceston where 75,000 people live, and for movement throughout the whole State, being centrally situated between the other two blocks of population: the towns on the North West Coast (50,000) and the capital, Hobart (120,000).

From the earliest days it was our conviction that students must be kept involved and concerned with the fundamental spiritual needs of the man in the street. We are not monastic, and training must take place in the context of needy people.

From 1960 onwards in our afternoons and days of prayer we trusted the Lord for openings for the students on a local weekly basis, and then for locations for evangelistic crusades of two or three weeks' duration towards the end of the school year.

It was not long before local churches were inviting us to help with Sunday schools and youth groups; and later, headmasters, constantly frustrated in carrying out the requirement of the Education Department in regard to Religious Instruction, were keen to make use of the students in the weekly sessions allotted to this subject. As one headmaster (now deceased) expressed it, "I don't want the clergy; I want your students because they

communicate with the pupils at their own level."
While certainly not joining the said headmaster in his
sentiments about the clergy, many of whom take a deep
interest in the work of the College, we are thankful for
the regard in which the work of the students is held,
and for the openings given, so vital for their own
development.

Each year we have had to take a very positive stand
of faith that there would be sufficient openings for the
students' evangelistic missions. Of course God has
answered prayer, but very often at the eleventh hour.
On one occasion we were very near the "deadline" and
were praying most authoritatively about this; as we
prayed, I was called out to meet a Presbyterian minister
from a country church thirty-five miles away. He had
come in with the specific purpose of asking us to send a
team of men to his three parishes!

As readers of *God's Smuggler* will remember, the
whole purpose of these missions is to develop the
students' initiative, sense of responsibility, and creative
faith. While we allot the teams a small amount of
money for initial expenses (two dollars per week per
head) we hope that this will be returned at the end of
the mission and that students will rise in faith to trust
God for the supply of all their needs.

Staff member and former student Jenny Davies
recalls:

"The four of us were half-way through our mission
in a rather poor suburb, and we were almost penniless.
We simply had to have money for petrol, food, and
such like. During one morning prayer time we asked
our heavenly Father for a gift to cover all these needs.
We only just mentioned it because we had so many
other things to pray about in the spiritual realm. We
were about to sit down to lunch when a knock was
heard at the door. It was a Christian rent-collector who

had called in during his rounds to see how we were getting on. (We were living in a church hall, so he wasn't looking for rent from us!) We invited him to share our meal, which really looked quite good even though we didn't know what the NEXT would be like! He refused politely and went his way. But fifteen minutes later he was back—God had clearly told him to turn back and give us six dollars.

"On another mission in a country area our car broke down and I took it to a local garage. It needed a new battery, valve grind and a few other things. We took a big leap of faith and told the mechanic to go ahead even though we had only a few dollars in hand towards the cost. Each day for four days I would go round to see him. He was most curious.

" 'Why did you come to a missionary training college?'

" 'How can you know you're in God's will?'

" 'What is your mission trying to do?'

"Finally he confessed he had accepted the Lord as a lad in Sunday School, but had never gone on.

"The day the car was ready (and we still had only the same few dollars) he said, 'Before you ask what this'll cost, I want to tell you that a local friend is paying for all the parts and I'm contributing the labour free of charge. Drive over to the pump and we'll fill up before you go.' "

Gordon McLean, now in Spain, gives these reminiscences:

"On our first mission with Devonport Presbyterian Church, one team member very brightly committed us to obtaining a Billy Graham film for Youth Night and a family film for Parents' Night. These, together with literature and so on, took our whole allowance of thirty dollars, so the mission was very much on faith. A crisis came when a bill arrived for five dollars twenty and all we had was the twenty cents. At 10 a.m. we prayed very definitely, claiming the promises and trusting to be able to pay it next day. At lunch time we visited all the shops, inviting the young people who served in them to come to our youth meeting the following Saturday night. Just outside one shop we met little old Miss Smith, a very keen Christian. She told us she had left an envelope for us at the church. When we opened it we found a five dollar note. That night I saw her at a meeting and thanked her for her faithfulness. When I told her that God had used her to answer a specific prayer request, she was thrilled and said, 'Isn't it wonderful. At 10 o'clock this morning I had no intention of giving you boys anything, but just about that time the Lord laid it on my heart that you needed five dollars so I put it in an envelope and took it down to the church.'

"One of the things we learned at College was not to read the Bible like a vacuum cleaner (catching everything but retaining nothing) but to look for definite promises, and claim them by faith. I asked God for a promise about the Hobart mission the next year, and He gave me John 15: 16, 'Go and bring forth fruit.' This fitted, because I wouldn't have chosen a place like a City Mission in which to work. I had also secretly hoped that neither of two other students would be on the team. Of course, I got both of them, and the job they did made me very thankful for them.

"We did see a miracle during the first week. It happened through Terry Walsh, an alcoholic whom Mr. Price and I had picked up on the street the year before, at which time he made a decision for Christ. Terry turned up at the mission service the first Sunday and after a session with us out in the kitchen went home fired with fresh enthusiasm for the Christian life. A couple of nights later he was given a lift by Don

Kellett. He witnessed to Don until 12.30 a.m., and also told him about us. Consequently, on the Thursday night Don turned up and when talking to me in the office admitted that he wanted what Terry had. He was a dried-out alcoholic. After pouring out his troubles for about an hour he attempted to walk out with a half-hearted promise to come back on Sunday. However, I felt it was really necessary to face him up with doing something about it then and there. He did, and has gone on with Christ ever since. It was a thrill to receive a tape from him recently.

"But by Thursday of the second week nothing more had happened and we were looking for the 'fruit that would remain.' There was a spare hour that evening before tea, so we spent it in prayer, and the revelation came to one of us that if He had promised then He had indeed committed Himself to bless.

"The next day a lady came to Christ on door-to-door visitation, so we were much encouraged. Friday night was Parents' Night, the last night in the children's 'Adventure Time' series. Attendance had been fairly small so the chances of getting many parents along looked very slim. However, we prayed and believed, and were later thrilled when the chapel was nearly full and several asked at the end of the meeting for literature about receiving Christ."

On one memorable afternoon of prayer at College we were all burdened about the lack of Gospel witness in many country areas of Tasmania. Dozens of schools had no regular Religious Instruction. (We knew of one country town of a thousand inhabitants that had only one Anglican service a month.) In many parishes liberal preaching had led to spiritual deadness and indifference; young people, if they did attend Sunday School of a sort, were drifting off in their early teens, with no intention of remaining within the church fellowship. What could be done?

Into the prayer time came a note of expectancy and daring. By God's grace we could do something about it . . . we *would* do something about it. Faith rose higher . . . high enough to surmount practical problems, lack of personnel, lack of provision, lack of a plan.

How Lord? And then the vision clarified. Why not a regular continuous scheme of country outreach by a small team of graduate students whose basic College training was complete but who needed further experience in evangelism?

But this would require mobile accommodation—a caravan, plus a big car to pull it. It would require the call of God to graduates to undertake such a ministry.

Yes! We took it from the Lord, and used the business letter terminology, "Thanking you in anticipation."

Quite quickly things began to move. Within two weeks there was a phone call from a Christian gentleman who lived nearby:

"Stewart, we have a caravan that we seldom use. I suppose we've lived in it for three or four weeks over the past eighteen months. Could you put it to use?"

Towards the end of the term, one of the students who was leaving—a young medical doctor—told me that the Lord had challenged him to leave his Holden Station Wagon behind for the Caravan Crusade.

After Graduation two of the graduates came to see me. One was a former accountant and the other a salesman. The Lord had spoken to them about country evangelism, and they wanted to be the "guinea pigs" for the Country Caravan Crusades.

So the Lord worked it out, and in February 1969 this movement commenced and has continued ever since. In the very first mission in a country area near the north-west coast, the lads met up with a keen Methodist minister who gave them full scope and the mission was terminated by a youth camp in which twenty-eight young people came forward for counselling.

God burdened hearts to support this work, and while, apart from one large gift at the commencement, the amounts have not been high, there has generally been enough in hand to support this operation without recourse to other monies. Many crusades have been conducted by both men and women students, even through the rough Tasmanian winter, and many young people won for Christ as a result.

How do local churches react to the outreach of the College? Some, of course, do not appreciate our conservative evangelical theology or our active evangelism, but some do, and much mutual blessing has resulted from close co-operation. Pastor Taylor of the Devonport Church of Christ writes:

"We recall how, with a great deal of hesitancy, we 'invited' the first W.E.C. team through. I had grave misgivings as to what I might be letting myself in for! It was indeed a 'faith' venture with a lot of hard praying that nothing would be said or done that might hinder the work here. However, I must say we have never looked back since that moment. It took a while for it to sink in but I gradually learnt, and applied, the principles of faith and living a victorious life in Christ. Whereas in the previous ministries it had largely been my doing something for the Lord, now it was making myself available for Him to do His work through me— a revolutionary concept that has changed my ministry and, I believe, has rubbed off on the church. In all the years since, we have never been disappointed in W.E.C., either in its message, students, or missionaries. We have the utmost confidence in its ministry—a long cry from that first hesitant 'launching'. In fact, we have found its ministry to be deep, lasting, sane and spiritual.

"What recollections we have of the first team! Jim Sterry's fine leadership, and the 'roasting' he gave the students for arriving back late one Sunday afternoon from a 'short drive' that developed into several hundreds of miles, at the invitation of one of my church members! The fine work done among the children in the children's meetings. The team's invitation to tea by a Christian doctor working at the hospital and the 'tour' of the hospital where, through the vital interest and witness of the youngest member, Alan King, the first seeds of the Gospel were sown that eventually led to the conversion of another doctor. The mysterious sickness that developed amongst the team until Mrs. Dinnen arrived and defined the 'disease' to be the result of too many cream cakes. The 'struggles' of Peter Belchamber whose testimony profoundly influenced our men, because they saw their own problems mirrored in his, and saw, too, a way through to victory.

"I must mention also the missionary vision imparted to the church through W.E.C. Over the years this interest had developed until three years ago in November we launched our Faith Giving Missionary Programme. In December, after giving several hundreds of dollars to the mission fields, we had about twenty dollars in the bank, and we faced a six weeks' tent mission at the end of January that was to cost in the region of $2,000. Yet this was adequately covered in one final thanksgiving offering. Altogether $2,500 went to the mission fields that year and it has increased each year since. Never once have we lacked on the home field. Many wonderful friendships with missionary partners have sprung up and prayer and financial support have developed steadily."

Of course, such a work of outreach and evangelism

simply could not survive apart from the faithful giving of God's humble stewards. The following testimony comes from a gracious saint of God who was very remarkably led on numerous occasions to help out students during their missions.

"When the first group of lads came to hold a mission it was summer, so they made use of our refrigerator for their meat, milk, etc. On one occasion I put a dozen eggs in it and told my husband that if I was out when they called not to forget to give the eggs to them. So one morning at about 7.30 a.m. Alan came for milk for breakfast and I said, 'Alan, here are a dozen eggs. Can you use them?' He looked rather sheepish and a grin came on his face. 'What's the joke?' I asked. He replied, 'I'll tell you a secret. We haven't anything for breakfast except bread and one of the boys said he wouldn't mind scrambled eggs as well.'

"Now I want to tell you one very special story—it happened later, on one of Peter Belchamber's weekend trips when he was training the Boys' Brigade officers. This incident thrills me yet, when I recall how the Lord spoke to me ever so plainly. One Friday morning as I got out of bed and stooped to put my slippers on, the word came through so plainly, I was amazed. 'I want you to give Peter $50 for a suit of clothes.' I said, 'Lord, that won't buy a suit of clothes.' But $50 was to be the amount. I said, 'Right, Lord. I'll go and get Your Word; give me a scripture to convince me I must tell him this is for a suit.' My Bible opened up to Zech. 3 : 4, 'And he answered and spake unto those that stood before him, saying, Take away the filthy garments from him. And unto him he said, Behold, I have caused thine iniquity to pass from thee, and I will clothe thee with change of raiment.'

"I said, 'Lord, that's terrific.' I was almost stunned

at how plainly the Lord can speak and make us understand.

"When my husband came in from feeding the fowls I told him what the Lord had told me and how He had confirmed His voice and orders for me in His Word. My husband said, 'Well, that's how it has to be; go and get the money ready for Peter tonight.' He duly arrived. I served his tea, and we sat and talked a bit. Then I said, 'The Lord spoke to me this morning in a miraculous way.' I told him what had happened, and read the verse of Scripture to him (because that was fantastic). He dropped his eyes, and I saw a tear fall. I knew then he had a problem, but I also thought he felt embarrassed at first, because I had stated a suit of clothes. But he said, 'Let us thank Him, shall we?' Then he opened his heart and told us his problem.

" 'I've been praying for that suit of clothes for three months. Mine is so tight and my pants are so threadbare, I'm always afraid the suit will split and give way when I am in the pulpit, and my coat is so tight I can't fold my arms or put any pressure on it at all.'

"Anyhow, Peter took his $50 and when in Launceston went to a men's wear shop to choose a suit. He found one that fitted beautifully, then he glanced at the price tag; it was $64. He was just taking it off when the proprietor came on the scene and said, 'That's a perfect fit.' Peter agreed but said humbly, 'It's a little more than I can pay.' 'Just a moment, aren't you from the Missionary College at St. Leonards?' asked the owner. Peter nodded. 'Oh well,' he said. 'I usually make deductions for you folks. Supposing I make it $56?' Peter recalled, 'I was just going to say that it was still too much when the Lord reminded me that I had six dollars in my other pocket.' So there were the fifty-six dollars, and the suit was his!

"Then the proprietor said, 'Leave the suit with us

for a week and I will have it specially pressed for you, as I guess in your work it will be packed in the suitcase quite a bit. Now go and choose a tie; that will be a gift from us.' "

Through pioneer country evangelism, Sunday School teaching, youth group leadership, door-to-door visitation, children's missions and religious instruction classes, many have found Christ over the past ten years, and many Christian young people have been challenged on the issue of true discipleship. Some have come to W.E.C. Others have gone elsewhere, but this does not concern us. Our one desire is to help young people discover the will of God, and to move in faith and obedience into the channel of His purpose, wherever that may lead.

7

Journeying

IT was obviously for the benefit of the Missionary Training College that staff should be willing to accept invitations to address conventions, churches, youth groups, and such like on the Australian mainland. While the main objective (and we had to be sure before the Lord about our own heart attitude in this) was service and ministry to others, opportunities were usually given to outline the work of the College and to challenge young people for Christian service and training.

These times have been adventures of faith for us, deepening our own experience of the Lord and enabling us to help others towards true discipleship.

On one journey, which occurred during school vacation, we Dinnens were able to travel as a family, taking the car on the overnight ferry between Tasmania and Melbourne. Just before leaving, a student came to me with an unusual request, "Mr. Dinnen, I feel the Lord wants you to have this money to give to anyone you meet who has a need." Never before or since has this happened.

However, on reaching Melbourne we were met by a married couple who had been students at the College and who were undergoing further technical training for the mission field. We had a short time of precious fellowship with them at the ferry terminal. When we were about to drive off, the Lord brought the money to mind and we gave them about ten dollars. They said

67

nothing but "Thanks!" at the time, but afterwards they wrote to say that their larder had been absolutely bare that day. They knew money was coming in a few days but they faced a bleak weekend—until the arrival of this supply, so lovingly arranged by the Lord through a student in college, sensitive to His prompting.

We drove off at noon, and as our final destination was Sydney, nearly 600 miles away, we were determined to travel as far as we possibly could that day. However, on reaching Wagga Wagga about 7 p.m., 260 miles from Melbourne, we had the distinct impression that we were meant to stop the night there. The only vacant accommodation was in a rather expensive hotel, and because of the heavy charge, we decided not to eat there, but to seek out a cheaper café for an evening meal. Imagine our feelings when, walking down the main street, we caught sight of two of our married graduates (now members of the Crusade) and their family, who were motoring from Sydney to a camp near the Victorian border. They had stopped for a short break and were about to drive off again westwards. They still had many miles to go that night. Quickly realising that we still had a few dollars left over from the amount given at College, we handed this over. Then we found out that they had had trouble with their car en route necessitating unforeseen expenses, and this amount was the Lord's further supply for them!

On another occasion I had been invited to Brisbane to speak each night at the Mt. Tamborine Christmas convention, which commenced on December 26th and went through to New Year's Day. (This is the time for summer holidays and conventions in the Southern Hemisphere.) On Christmas night I developed an intense abdominal pain. I had been a victim of these recurring bouts for over ten years, sometimes so fierce that if out driving I had to stop and find a place to lie out flat and wait until the pain subsided. At one stage this was diagnosed as ulcers, and diet had been adjusted accordingly. But this bout was an all-time special.

At 3 a.m. December 26th God challenged me to thank Him for this pain! After a long struggle there came a faint but sincere expression of thanks that this had happened. Next day the members of the W.E.C. fellowship had a prayer session round the bed and the pain receded. I was able to continue taking the convention ministry until the last meeting when again I was stricken. The local doctor arranged for a consultation with a specialist in Brisbane, who, it turned out, was a keen Christian. On completion of some very thorough tests he firmly announced that a non-functioning gall-bladder would have to be removed. However, since I was serving the Lord, he, too, would serve the Lord by removing the offending organ, free. Well, in spite of the pain, this was sweet music for a Scotsman, and two weeks later a successful operation was performed. It was good to realise the prayer of thanksgiving had gone up BEFORE the deliverance came! And what a complete and total deliverance it was.

In these tours it has been a thrill to see lives touched and directed by the Spirit of God.

In Perth, Western Australia, Doreen had a developing friendship with a young man, yet as the convention proceeded she had a growing awareness that God was asking her to put this on the altar and step out into missionary training. She serves God effectively now in West Africa—still single.

In Sydney, New South Wales, Ron was all set for a career in accountancy, but through facing up to simple but profound New Testament standards of surrender at a youth camp he "launched out into the deep", moved into missionary training, and is now headed for Africa.

69

Donald was a bank clerk on temporary duty in Hobart, Tasmania. He had already attended a W.E.C. Prayer Fellowship in Sydney and in an after-church fellowship in a home overlooking Sandy Bay, he listened intently as a team from the W.E.C. College had the privilege of challenging the young people to put their lives on the altar for God. In the leading of the Lord, linguistics and Bible translation came in for special emphasis and the issue which specially attracted Donald was the fact that we gave special linguistic training in our College. He came into training later, and recently returned from his first term in Chad where he has been working on the Tama language.

And so it could go on. There seems to be no special "key" in this kind of ministry of helping young folk become mobile for God—just a willingness to "get going" oneself and having a testimony to proving His faithfulness.

By 1967, the intensity of the programme, the inexorable demands of the College timetable, monthly public conferences, church services, State-wide representation for the Crusade, and incessant travel to fulfil interstate speaking engagements, were all beginning to take their toll. By this time, my wife had taken on outside responsibilities too. In addition to the demands of college life in which she supervised the catering, conducted lengthy correspondence with overseas graduate students, and had many counselling sessions with present students, she was now State chairwoman of the Australian Christian Women's Conventions (an interdenominational movement that is bringing many women under sound Biblical teaching), and conducted a weekly women's Bible Study which was attracting about fifty local ladies who felt the need for spiritual food. Apart from all this we were father and mother to two teenage daughters!

Frankly we needed a break, or to put it in proper academic terms, a "sabbatical".

It was during the first Tasmanian Keswick Convention at Port Sorell, Christmas 1966, that the Holy Spirit began to give us a growing awareness that 1967 was to be the year of the break. "Is this really from Your loving heart, Lord? Or are we dreaming it up out of our natural desire for a rest?" I remember making a bargain with God. "Lord, if You send me a reasonably sized gift, unmistakably marked for our personal use, within the next forty-eight hours, I'll take it You want us to have a break." Within the time limit we had a letter in the mail, postmarked Melbourne, and in it were $50 and a slip of paper that said, "For your personal use." No name, no address.

There was one snag—a giant forgery operation had just been uncovered in Melbourne and the bulk of the forged money was in ten dollar bills! But no, all was well and the money went into the bank without query. This was the first confirmation of the Lord's purpose.

As we thought round it we realised it would not be realistic to be away too long so we settled for eight weeks. But before reaching a final decision we felt the Lord had to do three things.

First, our daughters' education could not be interrupted. We needed to see God make it possible for them to be cared for, and not at College where the added responsibility on our younger staff would not be justified. Secondly, we felt that God could cause a suitably-equipped missionary couple to be home on furlough, and make them willing to act as stand-ins for us. Thirdly, the full financial provision was obviously necessary.

In each of these areas we saw the Lord work during the intervening weeks. Dr. and Mrs. Pippett, a Christian couple who with their family had recently come to

71

settle within a mile and a half of the College, graciously (and bravely!) offered to have Ruth and Grace. Mr. and Mrs. Don Barnes from Japan came on furlough, and their coming at that particular time was the result of several "impossible" miracles occurring on the field which released them six months earlier than originally planned. They were happy and willing to spend two months of their furlough at the M.T.C.

As for finance, we started to see gifts come in from all sorts of unexpected sources and the total crept closer and closer to the needed amount. On the night before we were due to pick up the tickets, we had $2,350—exactly fifty dollars short of the $2,400 needed for the tickets to U.S.A. and Britain and West Africa. Had God made a mistake? A Christian travel agent was to have the tickets ready next morning at 9 a.m.

We went for tea that night to the home where our daughters were going to stay. On returning to the College there was an envelope under our door with thirty dollars!

The next morning I left for town at 8 a.m. still twenty dollars short. I went first to the usual weekly prayer meeting of the Christian Business Men. On leaving this a brother handed me an envelope with some money in it and my heart leapt! The remaining need supplied? No. This brother's voice went on to say, "This is a gift for your missionaries in Indonesia."

"Oh well, thank You, anyway, Lord."

I stood outside, knowing that six blocks away and in fifteen minutes' time an agent was waiting for $2,400. I slowly drove the car round and stopped near the agency. However, before going in I felt impelled to say farewell to a dear brother in Christ with whom I had deep prayer fellowship over some personal problems he was facing. As soon as I went into his office he took the initiative. Instead of me asking how things were with him, he was asking me if I had any problems!

"How's your fare, Stewart?"

"Oh, ah, well, pretty good."

"What do you mean, 'pretty good'? Do you have it or not?"

"Oh, well, nearly there, you know."

"Stewart, tell me exactly how much you still require."

"You're cornering me now."

"Tell me."

"Twenty dollars."

"No problem," he said and with that he turned round to his cash box and took out two ten dollar bills.

Time—five minutes to nine.

"Lord, that was as close as I'd like it to be."

Apart from the three basic confirmations described, we had other encouragements in our planning. The very week we had planned to be in Philadelphia with our close American friends, was the week of the annual W.E.C. Staff Conference; we were invited to participate.

The very week we were to be in Scotland coincided with the start of the British W.E.C. holiday conferences at Kilcreggan; could we speak there too?

We felt led to plan a trip through West Africa in order to see our graduates in action on the field, and the five day period we had allotted to one particular field was the very time that all missionaries and national workers would be in conference—an ideal setting for obtaining an insight into field problems and conditions.

Two days after the final provision for our fare we were due to depart on a round-the-world tour with nothing but the tickets and a few dollars that had been specifically given for incidental expenses!

We proceeded as far as Sydney where I was due to speak at a weekend missionary convention in a suburban

Baptist Church, and out of this came further provision from the Lord. But the big deliverance for all our incidental expenses came in a surprising way. During our four day stop-over in Auckland, a letter from West Australia, forwarded from the College, reached us and in it was a letter and a cheque. The letter was from the widow of one of our former students. They had had a year's training with us, intending to go to the mission field, but owing to financial difficulties in the husband's family he had felt obliged to return home and work on the farm. There he was tragically killed in a ghastly tractor accident. Months later, after the release of the estate, the young widow had sent us a very large gift as an appreciation of their time at College, and we were to use it for personal needs.

So the great "safari" proceeded. After renewing home base contacts in U.S.A. and Britain, it was the thrill of our lives to visit graduates of both British and Australian training centres, in Switzerland, Senegal, The Gambia, Liberia, Ivory Coast, Ghana and South Africa. It would be unfair to mention some and not others. But all, by their continuing presence on the field, are living testimonies to the sustaining and enabling power of the Spirit when He is liberated in disciplined lives.

It was thrilling also to realise that graduates were the channels for God to reproduce these principles in national disciples. Not all of our fields are advanced to this point yet, but the different degrees to which the national church has advanced gave us some rich illustrative material for future teaching sessions. We studied the "first fruits" stage in Senegal and Gambia, the newly-emerging churches in the Ghana field, the growing maturity of the missionary-guided congregations in the Ivory Coast, and had just a glimpse of the fully autonomous churches of Liberia.

A united conference in one field revealed some of the problems missionaries face, and strengthened our determination that a much wider knowledge and experience of church affairs was needed before proceeding overseas.

Problem 1: An evangelist wants to have more free time and adequate facilities for learning French. But the missionaries who trained him in the Bible School know (a) that he does not have the capacity for learning it to a satisfactory degree, and (b) that to speak French is a "status symbol". Problem 2: An evangelist wants to go back to Bible School for more training. The elders agree. But the missionaries ask, "Who will pay for him?" If the church does, then who will pay for another evangelist to do his work? The church cannot face it, on present levels of giving. Problem 3: Some churches put their members under discipline for sending their children to a Roman Catholic school; some churches do not. Who is right? Problem 4: The evangelists object to a missionary discouraging churches in America from sending gifts directly to the national workers' fund. Does the story of the Good Samaritan not justify the weak receiving help from the strong?

We returned wiser and more convinced than ever, not merely from our own observation but from the consensus of opinions expressed, that the final answer in every field is not quantity but quality; not larger numbers of missionaries or greater material supply or more academic knowledge, but disciples who, by example and teaching, can beget disciples.

8

Fruitbearing

TRAINING, in our estimation, is not training unless it results in people who will go through with God to the field, stay there and produce fruit. We are not simply a Bible Institute which offers a course, and whose responsibility ends when the graduate packs his bag and leaves with a neatly-lettered certificate in his pocket. If we are training disciples there will be discipleship: not self-pleasing, not settling down to self-centred living in an affluent society.

While we can rejoice in the dozens who have gone through with God we certainly do not want to give the impression that we have consistently been on the victory side. We are so very fallible, and no less so than when it comes to dealing with lives. When we fail to help students reach a place of release and effectiveness we are jogged into a fresh realisation of the nature of this spiritual warfare, and the ease with which it is possible for us to move out of the place of total faith-dependence on the Lord.

We have failed others on a fellowship level and they have left us, feeling grieved at what they consider to be a wrong attitude on our part.

Some who never reached a sphere of fruitful ministry have since written to us with regrets, some with remorse and some even with repentance. How easy it is to be side-tracked. Several years after their graduation we received a letter from one couple. The husband wrote:

"I remember how often during Bible Studies Mr. Dinnen used to bring out the dangers of bearing a grudge, and yet this is the trap that seems to have caught me. I felt that we were sinned against, and consequently we were deeply offended and have borne a grudge ever since. Yet, somehow, especially with yourselves and college, there has been a deep link of fellowship which binds you to us . . .

"We seem to have been shelved . . . not useless, just put to one side, and, although we have had wonderful opportunities to witness, not once since we left college have we led a soul to the Lord Jesus.

"Our hearts often break with thoughts of those joyous years spent at the Master's feet while at college. Out of a sincere heart I want to ask your forgiveness for bearing a grudge . . .

"It seems the past few years have been almost wasted time. It is as though we've been 'grounded'. The aircraft is O.K. Everything works. We can start the engines and taxi to the runway, but can't get cleared for take-off."

Yet, just a day or two before the above letter arrived, a local high school teacher, a vital witnessing Christian, had written saying, "How I thank God for W.E.C. and for 'X' (naming the writer of the letter quoted above) who, when he was a student, led me to Christ and set my feet on the right track."

No, it is not all a success story. Witness this extract written nearly four years after leaving College.

"My real purpose in writing is to tell you that the Lord has been dealing with me concerning sin that has been in my heart, in some cases for years, and I now find, although He has forgiven, I need to write to you as head of the Staff to ask forgiveness for the bitterness and worse I have felt towards you all since I left. Please forgive me—I can assure you things are seen in

77

a far different light now and in fact I ought to thank you for what you tried to do for us during our time at college. May God bless you."

On the bright side, a stream of letters testifies to triumph out of trial, to peace in the midst of problems, to inner steadiness in the face of Satanic opposition.

Writing from the candidate orientation course, which is the normal "next step" after graduation for those intending to join W.E.C., a former student, John Snedden, now in Sumatra, wrote:

"Well, here I am at Headquarters, trusting in Christ . . . boy, I dare do no other! I felt scared that I'd do the wrong thing, but who really wants to back out? Not me. I thank God that He has let me come into W.E.C. I know you should only be proud of Christ, yet I feel also so proud of C. T. Studd and Mr. Grubb. How I trust the Lord that He will give grace to accept what they accepted so that I may gain Christ and see Him save people.

"It's funny—I want to thank you all for what you taught me by word and by example during the two years at M.T.C. but we thanked the Lord for that. Is it that I can thank you for the same thing? No. But I thank you that you were faithful so that He might impart grace and life to others."

Robin Hadfield, now in Sumatra, wrote these lines after completing his candidate course in Auckland, New Zealand:

"There are so many pitfalls. I've titled this: 'Many a Slip between M.T.C. and the Ship.'

"First, the pull of the world. Fashions and 'things' can still capture the heart. Even T.V. in the home can be a snare. It is so easy to fall in line and waste precious hours.

"Then affections. I was kneeling beside my bed and a verse leapt at me from Proverbs. 'Above all else guard your affections. For they influence everything else in your life.' The Lord was speaking directly to me . . . my affections were getting out of hand. My mind had been racing away dreaming of all sorts of unchecked thoughts . . . everything out of proportion. Conviction led to confession and cleansing.

"Then the mind can be a real battlefield. It is so easy to see . . . desire . . . imagine. Experience has proved that there must be a daily practical outworking of bringing every thought into captivity to the obedience of Christ. Someone has said, 'Never have a vacant mind.'

"Rest. I went through long periods of uncertainty regarding the future. As time ticked by, I began to fret and become agitated instead of resting in the power of the living Word of God and what He had promised.

"Then doctrine. Doctrine divides. This is what I found. Dogmatically thumping my pet theory forces fellowship to fly out of the window. The Lord brought someone of the opposite viewpoint across my path and I found it hard to show real love in my heart towards him, especially when he pressed home his beliefs on a certain issue. But I failed too, in that I allowed the Devil to poison my mind against my brother instead of showing real Holy Ghost love. But, praise the Lord, towards the end of our time of fellowship together we saw the Lord work in both our hearts, developing a real love and concern for each other."

And what of field situations? From Thailand, Ian and Patsy Cook wrote:

"Ian was held up and robbed a month ago. Six bandits armed with shotguns relieved him of his new motor bike, watch, spectacles, shoes and almost everything else. He was glad they left him his trousers at least! How he managed to get home without his specs I don't know.

"I was dealing with a Thai girl recently over the matter of spirits. I felt as if I'd been held over the mouth of hell . . . later I was oppressed by a terrible heaviness and stark horrible fear. I shared it with Ian and he produced his usual cure—the Word. Hallelujah! As I told him each lie that the serpent was whispering he would get an appropriate portion of Scripture and read it in a nice clear voice. (It was around midnight.) In a most amazing way the bonds went snapping one after the other until there was complete release. What a Saviour!"

Don and Diane Dick wrote from Chad:

"The Devil is active. I remember once Diane and I both awoke separately about 2 a.m. sensing a fearsome presence of evil. We could 'see' the evil darkness and feel it around us, and only the prayer of simple faith and pleading for the protection of Jesus' blood freed the air and we could go back to sleep.

"We have a fourteen-year-old girl helping Diane. She was recently divorced from her Mohammedan husband and now fends for herself and her five-month-old son. It is not certain yet whether this little mite will suffer from the horrible effects of congenital syphilis. It is heart-breaking to see the havoc Islamic licence brings into the home. I remember studying this religion at M.T.C. and being struck with the permitted perversion which prevails in the Muslim world, but it is only when you have actual access into the culture and homes that the horror of it is really felt."

Victory is praise in adverse circumstances. From Colombia, South America, Peter Horrell wrote these lines:

"My new quarters are unique. I have a roof that makes the slightest drizzle outside sound like a raging thunderstorm inside, a toilet that does not work, and the kind of neighbour who thinks that the whole town wants to listen to her radio.

"The staple diet seems to be potatoes. Potato soup in fatty grease for breakfast; again for dinner and again for the evening meal. I enjoy the last spoonful most!

"Yesterday I went to the local market when the small group of believers had an open air service. As I watched them fearlessly preach Christ before several hundred interested people, and saw the response that followed, I lifted up my heart to the Lord and thanked Him for bringing me to Colombia. May He be able to fulfil His purpose in and through me, in this land."

Before going to Venezuela, Ken and Joy Watson wrote from Spanish language school in Texas:

"Last week we had our mid-term exams—they certainly know how to give exams here too! We praise the Lord that He enabled us to pass in each subject. We do not find it easy, but as we look back we are certainly grateful for the discipline and spiritual principles which are taught at M.T.C. for we need to put them into practice here where the pressure is ON!"

Maurice Charman gives this intimate picture from Taiwan:

"It is 9 p.m. and I sit just in my shorts enjoying the cool blast from the fan. This is the only way to escape the present 90° temperature and 95° humidity. The breeze generated by the fan does much to relieve the situation but with this blessing comes a minor frustration—my loose papers are being blown around the room. What to do? Turn off the source of comfort or do something about the papers? Rest easy; a few makeshift paper-weights soon have all in order—a fishing float, a padlock, a wooden block puzzle and so on.

"Reviewing almost three years' service here in Taiwan the above example seems to illustrate the

81

situation very well. The Lord has blessed us with His presence and cooling touch but, as is always the case when we are in touch with Him, a few loose edges are ruffled. What has been the answer? Is it to turn off the source of blessing? Definitely not. What then? Simply allow the Lord to apply His paper-weights to our loose edges. So often I've felt the Lord's weights upon me—a waiting time, or uncertainty—these are things I find difficult to take. But so it must be, otherwise the only alternative is to turn off the source of blessing.

"The camps here have been a real blessing and encouragement. At one, attended by 320 senior boys and girls, I led the devotional times (all in Chinese). On the last evening round a camp fire, seven stood to acknowledge Christ as Saviour and another twenty to show their willingness to follow the Lord in true discipleship."

From Japan, graduate Elaine Henderson writes:

"Our battle here is spiritual pressure. There is not an 'evil' atmosphere such as I've heard of elsewhere. It's more elusive than that. It's almost as if Satan works under a cloak. The enemy doesn't hold his captives in chains of iron but in cords of silk, deceptively weak in appearance and yet terribly strong. Even those who show earnest interest just can't seem to break through. Of the infinitesimally small number who do, a heart-breaking number fall away. I need to know a much higher level of power in prayer if I'm ever going to be effective. There seems to be a tremendous barrier to get through, but hallelujah for the glorious victory of Jesus! All I can do is to hold on to this in 'cold blood' at times."

Holding on in "cold blood" . . . doesn't sound conspicuously triumphant, yet as one outstanding spiritual leader once confided:

"I don't have 'big' victories. I just get through . . . just by the skin of my teeth."

Here, finally, is an extract from a young lass who passed through M.T.C., went to India, and in a few years was taken to be with the Lord whom she so desperately longed to serve effectively. Deidre Cornish battled every inch of the way. The glory of it is simply that she never gave up, and in spite of battles in the most intense areas of all—the spirit and the mind—she held on to God for ultimate victory.

"India has become very much my home. I have a growing affection for our Indian brothers and sisters, and there certainly is beauty amidst the dirt and flies. One outstanding thing is the love and affection for one another, shown on this field. True, as a fellowship we do not always agree, but underneath is a loving understanding which is very vital.

"Things have not been easy. At first I did not understand what was going on, but certainly God used it to prune and expand. There were failures in language exams, discouragement, almost despair. (Would it ever come? But it has!) There was sickness. Then learning to live with people from different countries. These Americans! (They're not so bad after all.) No one seems to notice the language student . . . nothing exciting happens . . . just the daily grind. Everyone else is praising the Lord for blessing, but I CAN'T EVEN COMMUNICATE! Travelling alone was a nightmare (although not any more). There was disappointment in a love affair. Then came the frightening experience of depression and an overwhelming urge to end it all.

"In L. there is a Christian doctor and his wife—'super' Christians from America with a deep personal experience of the Lord. For seven months now I have been receiving help from them, and at last life and the

83

Christian life are beginning to make sense. Never would I have desired it to have been this way, and yet I can just praise God for His enabling, leading and growing.

"I have a new love and understanding for other people. Many prejudices have broken down. I find myself desiring the fellowship of others and able to give myself in a new way, almost unconsciously.

"Spiritually I am not where I thought I was—just very human, but finding God to be enabling in a new way. 'I can't—He must.' I have a deep desire for my faith to be a reality, to meet the demands of every-day life, and with it the desire to share it as such a reality, not in words but in life."

It was only a matter of months after writing these lines, that the Lord took her to be with Himself after a sudden and severe illness. Deidre leaves a fragrant memory, but to us she is more than a memory, she is a symbol—a symbol of the triumph of spirit over flesh—of the Christ-life over the self-life. Oppressed with fears and tensions to a degree greater than the average missionary, she went through in the revealed will of God, refusing defeat and refusing to turn and flee.

She was a disciple.

9

Timing

IS it right to have faith "targets" and "deadlines" in the work of the Lord? Isn't this too humanistic? Isn't it trying to pour God into our little bottle?

Maybe it is the opposite—God pouring us into His bottle!

The simple and over-riding fact is that targets and deadlines seem to work. And if they work, consistently and practically, surely we must acknowledge that God is behind them.

One of the most helpful books on this topic comes from the pen of Norman Grubb. It has the catching title *Touching the Invisible*.* In it he recounts how the W.E.C. Headquarters fellowship became more and more concerned about the paramount need of discovering God's will before daring to declare their faith.

*Published by Lutterworth Press, London.

"So it became impressed more and more on us that effectual praying must be guided praying: that the first essential was not to pray, but to know what to pray for: that special and clear provision has been made for this in the Scriptures, when Paul said in Romans 8: 26, 27 that the Spirit is given expressly to guide our praying; for true prayers are God's prayers prayed through us—they issue from God's mind, are taught us of His Spirit, are prayed in His faith, and are thus assured of answer. On this basis our meetings took a new form. Guidance must be found. We must go to our knees only when

85

we know from God for what we are going. To obtain this, formality, time limits, and human control must go.

"The entire household gathers at 9 a.m., anything from twenty-five to forty of us. The objective of the meetings is entirely practical, not a study of doctrine nor a Bible reading, but the tackling of the immediate problems of the work. It may concern a number of new recruits for the fields and the need of finance for them: the granting of a Government permit to open a new area of work: a tribe unyielded to the Gospel: a difficulty between workers. The matter is outlined and discussed. Opinions and criticisms are invited. Gradually the conviction gains ground among us all that such and such an outcome would glorify God—a certain sum of money by a certain date; a move of the Spirit at a certain place; the granting of an official permit; a reconciliation. The Scriptures are then examined. What examples have we as a ground for our faith? We turn to David, Daniel, Moses, Paul. Were they sure of their guidance? Did they believe and declare it? Did it come to pass? Can we fairly compare our situation to theirs? If so, then—and only then—we pray, believe, receive, declare our faith and persist, with all the authority of the Master's words, 'Whosoever shall *say*' (the word of command, much stronger than 'pray') 'unto this mountain, Be thou removed . . . and shall not doubt in his heart, but shall believe that those things which he saith shall come to pass; he shall have whatsoever he saith.' "

In the development of the Training Centres, both in Glasgow and Tasmania, we have sought to work towards the discovery of the Lord's will on a fellowship basis—the "fellowship" consisting, basically, of the staff who carry the responsibility of the work and, whenever practical, the students, so that they learn the ways of the Spirit. Indeed, there have been times when the students have taken the initiative in discovering and declaring a faith target and we staff have found ourselves following. This is the exception, of course, but Scripture does not preclude it. Young Samuel had a revelation from God that was beyond Eli's knowledge. Paul tells Timothy not to be embarrassed over his youthfulness.

In praying through for one of our early Easter conventions we were surprised when one of the women students committed herself by saying, "We expect you to save three souls at our convention, Lord." Other students took this up, and soon there was unanimous and authoritative praying along this one line.

Is this not just mob-psychology? We prefer to assert that if the Holy Spirit is a real person, and is capable of impressing on our spirits the desire or "the burden of the Lord", as the Old Testament prophets called it, then the easy development of a unified conviction in the fellowship is an indication that He is at work. So we staff joined in—rather slowly in this case, because we have looked on our conventions not so much as evangelistic efforts as teaching seminars for growing Christians.

Anyway, the three souls were saved. The third was actually converted while travelling by car to her home eighty miles away after the convention. But the Holy Spirit was using what she had learned during it. Her father was a Methodist minister and rejoiced in the good news. Later our own daughter Grace was converted under his ministry while she was on holiday with some friends in that area.

But returning to targets, we have had to trust the Lord consistently regarding applications to the College. Since we are attached to a missionary organisation young people think twice and three times before committing themselves to a programme like ours. The more general Bible training given at other colleges is more attractive and offers greater scope, leading to more widely-recognised qualifications. The real battle-ground is in regard to men. On numerous occasions we have been distinctly impressed with a particular number of new male applications that we should expect in a new intake. Towards the end of one college year, around November, we were clearly impressed by the figure of ten men—a human impossibility, since we were then in touch with only three or four, and the bulk of applications are usually in hand long before that time. But God worked a miracle and ten men joined us. The joy of it was that we had already declared our faith in our public rally that month. When the February meeting came round what a thrill it was to ask those ten men to stand so that all could see the faith target now "in the visible".

Does God meet "deadlines"? When the deadline itself is a revelation from God, then we are only agreeing with what He Himself has decreed. Someone has likened prayer to the switch in an electrical circuit. The power is always available but only flows on completion of the circuit by the switch. Norman Grubb used to say, "The existence of a need is evidence of God's intention to supply."

One of God's blessings to us has been Len. He is a twentieth century Barnabas; he owned land but sold it and brought the money to the disciples' feet. When it came his turn to depart for overseas, a very large amount was needed—a fare to London, money for a year's stay there while he took the course at the Missionary School of Medicine, and the onward fare to West Africa. A few weeks before the sailing date much was still required. Are sailing dates God's deadlines? Again we proved the reality of knowing and receiving, and he left "on schedule" with every need supplied.

Surely the key is awareness and authority. If we

live closely to Him we soon learn to recognise His guidance and this certain knowledge puts authority into our praying. It is not merely asking and hoping but knowing and receiving.

Sometimes in the development of our building programme we have been challenged to set a deadline for the completion of a part. Not only does this develop faith muscles but usually leads to good healthy physical muscles as well!

One such project was the erection of an office block and residential apartment—a total of seven rooms. Splendid help from Christian friends saw us well on the way, but internal finishing is always a laborious process for amateurs, and, of course, with student help limited to six hours per week, progress was painfully slow. But we felt urged to believe that it could be finished and dedicated at our October month-end public rally. Many unforeseen snags occurred in the intervening weeks, but unforeseen help came too, in the form of the parent of one of our young staff members. He was a skilful joiner and completed much of the office furniture.

On the day of dedication, however, we still had two cupboards to complete and time was running out; the dedication ceremony was to be that afternoon. At 11 a.m. a Christian business man, an insurance assessor with a flair for carpentry, drove in, having left home sixty-five miles away at 9.30 a.m. He quickly took up the tools, and by 3 p.m. the offices were respectable enough for a dignified dedication.

From the little State of Tasmania we have seen a growing number of young people going to the mission field. Their departures are always times of rejoicing, and of deep spiritual challenge to other young people. But the added responsibility for them comes upon us home-staffers—not legally, nor even organisationally, but in that indefinable way that can only be described as "fellowship"; so we seek to take a stand of faith that from their home State their financial support will be regularly supplied. Year by year we have seen this figure grow commensurate with the need. In fact, we have a monthly TARGET and a monthly DEADLINE to be met, and consistently this is provided from the giving of Christian friends and churches, without publicity, appeals or hints.

Time after time we come near to the end of the month and the target has not been achieved, but, as we express positive faith expectantly and determinedly before the Lord, He supplies—often in the last day. Is there a law of "holy desperation"? We think there is! And we think we are in good company—Jacob at Jabbok, or Hezekiah in Jerusalem, with Rabshakeh taunting him over the city wall!

On one occasion we were approaching the end of a term and it had become obvious that the old coke-fuelled stove would need extensive repairs which could be done only in holiday time when there was no large family to feed. Careful examination showed that possibly $200 would be needed. At the same time we were informed that the supply of coke would cease in the not too distant future. The last straw was a promised increase in its price meantime.

It was clear that this was the moment to install a different type of stove, and the answer was obviously to switch to gas. However, it would cost over $1,000 for purchase and installation of stove, gas lines, cylinders, etc. We went ahead with a firm order, with a specific request that it be installed before the second term began. The gas company were most co-operative, but would the Lord "co-operate"?

An elderly lady, recently converted and already

appreciating the spiritual nourishment at my wife's weekly Bible Class, was growing in grace and sorting out the issues of her unconverted days. One of these was her possession of brewery shares. She became so uncomfortable about these that she called Marie aside one day and asked:

"What project are you working on just now, my dear?"

"We're in the process of arranging for a gas stove."

"What will it cost?"

"Why do you ask?"

"I want to help."

"But we can't allow you to face such a heavy bill as that. Perhaps you would like to share . . ."

"Just send the bill to me—the *total* bill—when it comes in."

We reached another deadline regarding worn out equipment during 1969, when our ancient Farmall "A" tractor broke down. We naturally raised the matter in our afternoon of prayer. Meanwhile we had been having the temporary use of a diesel tractor owned by a Christian farmer whose son was now with W.E.C. on the mission field. But we had so much to do we felt we could not go on using his on a loan basis. It occurred to us that, since this brother had recently sold his farm, he might be willing to sell the tractor. Its value was about six or seven hundred dollars (another friend had bought a similar second-hand model recently and paid this amount for it). But we had nothing in the region of that sum in hand. What were we to do?

About the same time we received a gift of $200 to be used as we saw fit. The Lord clearly impressed me that I should telephone this gentleman and ask him if he were willing to sell.

"Look, this little tractor of yours we've been using—would you consider selling it?"

"Yes, Stewart, I don't need it now that I'm away from the farm."

"What do you want for it?"

"What do you want to offer me for it?"

"Well, I would rather you just tell me what you feel you should have for it, and we, ah, can think about it."

"Well," he said. "The Lord has spoken to me about this and He told me you were going to ask to buy it and He also told me the price I had to ask for it."

"And what was that?"

"Two hundred dollars."

"Praise the Lord! That's just the amount we have!"

It might be said, "It's all right for you to trust the Lord, but is it right to bring up children in such an 'insecure' atmosphere? Is it not putting an unnecessary strain on them?"

We have never found it so—in fact, God's timings and supply specifically for them have been a tremendous blessing and encouragement to us, as a family.

The very week we had to make a decision regarding whether to send Ruth to a public school or private (fee-paying) school, we were approached by a Christian lady who said, "God has told me to give $100 towards Ruth's education." This was God's seal that she should go to the private school, which for a number of important and personal reasons was better suited to Ruth's need.

As each term has come around and the need has had to be met, God has provided. The lady who was led to give the first gift was never led to give any more for that purpose. God wanted to keep us looking simply to Him alone!

One might ask, "Do things always work out like this? Are there not times when the deadline has not been met, the target not 'hit', the provision not supplied?"

We must admit that this has happened, and our only explanation is our own human fallibility in not sensing the true purpose of the Lord.

On one occasion we were particularly concerned about adequate facilities for the development of our youth work. The obvious answer seemed to be the provision of a camp site. Some time after reaching what we felt was a place of faith about this, a Christian businessman offered us four acres of land in a good country location. It was bounded by a crystal-clear rivulet which would have given a perfect water supply and electricity was available close by. But this acreage was too small for development. We offered to buy more land from a nearby farmer; he was willing to let it go for the price of the taxes which he had had to pay for it over the past few years—a ridiculously small amount. But the owner of a strip of land between the farmer's property and the four acres first offered adamantly refused to sell. The project was quite impracticable without this. The whole scheme fell through.

Was our faith false? Did the Christian businessman offer out of the will of the Lord? Did Satan oppose us through the intractability of the third owner?

Just recently we failed to reach our monthly target for missionary support. We were relieved when one of the number, studying in Switzerland, wrote to say he had taken a job during that month, because the language school had closed for the summer vacation! But what about the others on our list? We know that with our Mission's sharing system they would not lack basic essentials, but why had this happened? Had we been taking things for granted? Were we becoming coldly accustomed to others' sacrificial giving?

To give a full and fair picture we also have to admit that it is much easier to pray through to the point of faith for material goals than for spiritual.

We have a vivid recollection of a married student for whom we had a deep spiritual concern. He was so dogmatic—completely unapproachable on some issues of doctrine, forceful and demanding in his family relationships. Time and again we tried to believe for his release, but it never came.

Another young man was so full of pride. Everyone but himself could see it, and we hoped and prayed for a revelation to his own heart. But it never came, at least to our knowledge, and he never joined the Crusade.

Were we lacking in faith? Were we lacking in love? How far can we go in expecting a basic change of disposition? After twenty-two years in this kind of work we still do not have all the answers.

And yet we confidently and joyously assert that time after time we do see lives transformed, outlooks changed, deliverances accomplished, victories won. We have seen parents' attitudes reversed, suspicious ministers become sympathetic, and church situations altered, because of creative faith based on the assurance of God's revealed will.

So we must be honest. No, not inevitably or automatically can faith targets, once adopted, be realised. Nevertheless in the over-all picture there is a clearly discernible pattern in which, through serious-minded sensitivity to the Lord's purpose, and through creative faith, we "touch the invisible" and it becomes, in His time, visible.

10

Expounding

WHAT is the theory behind the practice? What is the key to deliverance? What is the secret of effectiveness? What lies behind creative faith? What principles undergird constructive fellowship?

No missionary can help build a church on New Testament standards unless he or she knows the truth of deliverance working in the life. "The truth shall make you free." What truth? Simply the realisation that God sees the old "you" as finished in the Cross, and a new "you" alive in the resurrection life of Christ, and therefore capable of infinite possibilities.

What happened at the Cross? Many simply say, "Jesus died for my sin", and this is true, but Scriptures like Colossians 3: 3 say "You died", and 2 Corinthians 5: 17 says we are a "new creation". Of course, our feelings often do not allow us to accept this and, manfully honest, we say, "If I feel like this then I'm not going to be hypocritical enough to say that my old nature has gone!" Is there not a danger in using the term "nature"? Scripture does not use it in this connection. Paul wisely talks about the "old man" and the "new man". Paul is not speaking about a state but about a relationship. Obviously what we are meant to see is that as we walk in active faith, asserting, in spite of feelings, the reality of the new relationship, we are in a position to overcome. If the relationship is positively maintained, we are able to resist evil. As James Denney says, "As long as faith is at the normal tension

95

the life of sin is inconceivable." Faith in what? Faith in the dynamic and radical change that the New Birth affects. Not without strong reason did Paul give several vivid, telling, profound metaphors regarding our union with Christ in His death and resurrection. Romans six says we were co-buried (v. 4); we were co-planted (v. 5); we were co-crucified with Him (v. 6); that having died with Christ we shall co-live with Him (v. 8).

Verses 1-11 of Romans six are directed to the spiritual understanding—"know" (vv. 3, 6, 9), "believe" (v. 8), "reckon" (v. 11); verses 12-23 are directed to the will—"yield" (vv. 13, 16), "obey" (vv. 16, 17), "serve" (vv. 16, 17, 18, 19, 20, 22). Far too quickly we plunge in trying to apply our will in the drive for holiness, but with little success, because we remain unenlightened regarding the significance of the "having-been-delivered" relationship.

Instead we need first of all to grasp, appropriate, accept with the spiritual understanding, all the benefits of the new relationship. From this "advanced position" we now will to resist, achieve, overcome; and we can, not because of anything we ourselves may do, but by understanding the advantageous position into which we have been placed when we came to Christ.

When a new recruit joins the Army he is given the full equipment of an infantry soldier—but he has no idea of all the resources of fire power that are available to him, and to his platoon, until they are demonstrated to him in simulated battle conditions. I may not have realised, when I came to Christ, all the tremendous resources that are in Him but as I appropriate Scriptural truth I come to see, to know, to experience, the power of His resurrection Life. The spiritual principle of Life-in-Christ-Jesus sets you free from the principle of sin-and-death (Rom. 8: 2).

For years, even after joining W.E.C., I struggled

to "reckon" myself "dead" to sin. But it would not work. Ted Hegre of Bethany Fellowship, Minneapolis, was the man whom the Lord used to open my eyes. I saw that "reckon" did not mean "pretend" but "accept-it-as-an-actual-fact".

"Dead" in Scripture never means "annihilated" but "separated from". God told Adam and Eve that if they partook of the fruit of a certain tree they would die. They did: they were separated from God and had no life-giving union with Him. As Christ died once-for-all, He came out from under the demand of death which the law makes for sin (He had become sin for us); so, too, we are to take it as a fact that we have come out from under (dead, or died out to) sin and are alive in Jesus Christ our Lord (Rom. 6: 9–11).

All this brought a new release to my spiritual life. Without it I had really very little to give to the students. With it, I found a principle that, when applied, "produced the goods".

James Denney says in *The Death of Christ** (page 106):

"The very same experience in which a man becomes right with God, that is, the experience of faith in Christ who died for sins, is an experience in which he becomes a dead man so far as sin is concerned and a living man (though this is but the same thing in other words) so far as God is concerned. . . . Faith is an attitude and act of the soul in which *the whole being* is involved, and it is determined through and through by its object."

As regards effectiveness, the only Effective One in the spiritual realm is the Holy Spirit. Therefore, the only effective servant of Christ is the one who is under the control of the Spirit and through whom the Spirit thus has liberty to express Himself.

* Published by Tyndale Press, London.

In relation to the believer there is a three-fold ministry of the Spirit—what He does **for** us, what He does **in** us and what He does **through** us.

In the first, we are the object of His activities. He guides us (Rom. 8: 14), He leads us into truth (John 16: 13), He assures us that we are the children of God (Rom. 8: 16), He enables us in prayer (Rom. 8: 26), He convicts of sin (John 16: 8), He strengthens us (John 16: 7), and so on.

In the second activity of the Spirit we are the area of His activities, and the nine-fold fruit of the Spirit (Gal. 5: 22–23) come into action within our personality in three distinct relationships: first in ourselves—joy, peace, self-control, goodness; then in our relationship to others—love, patience, gentleness, meekness; and thirdly in our relationship to God—faith.

In the third activity of the Spirit we are the channels or agents for the expression of the gifts released through us in the service of the Church. Whereas the fruit of the Spirit is the life of God *in* us, the gifts of the Spirit are the work of God *through* us.

Four lists of gifts are given in the New Testament and no two lists are the same—an indication of the freshness and originality of the Spirit. He cannot be bound by fixed lists! Quickly surveying Romans 12, 1 Corinthians 12: 7–10 and 28, and 1 Peter 4: 10–11, we see a further three-fold subdivision—service in edification (Wisdom, Knowledge, Exhortation, Teaching and Prophecy), service in practical affairs (Helps, Leadership, Administration, Faith, etc.), and service when the phenomenal or supernatural is needed (Healing, Miracles, Discernment of Spirits, Tongues, Interpretation of Tongues). All Christians have at least one gift ("Each hath received *a* gift"—1 Pet. 4: 10 R.V.).

Perhaps a word of explanation is needful here, because mention of the gifts of the Spirit raises evangelical "hackles" in many countries. W.E.C. does not major on the third subdivision (the phenomenal) but neither does it rule it out. In some of our exceptionally hard mission fields, an expression of a phenomenal gift has opened the door to an otherwise unresponsive people. We abide by the Pauline evaluation of seeking the best gifts, and those that edify, rather than the phenomenal, but we would be sticking our heads in the sand if we completely denied the validity of these gifts for today, when God is manifestly working along these very lines in many parts of the world.

Returning to the general topic of the empowering of the Spirit, it seems abundantly obvious from the Acts that effectiveness is wholly dependent on being "filled". Indeed a careful study of the context of nearly every mention of the filling of the Spirit will reveal a significant pattern: fulness, service, and effectiveness.

We have constantly held before our recruits the supreme necessity of coming to terms with God on the matter of His fulness. We do not prescribe that each must have the same experience, but we consider it scriptural to challenge, exhort, and teach the students about the necessity of being filled with the Spirit, and about having a settled conviction on a scriptural basis for their position and experience.

God meets some quietly and unobtrusively; for many it is a by-faith entering in, by a realisation, after teaching, of the total adequacy of the fulness of Christ ministered to us in His Holy Spirit; for some it is a radical and even emotional experience; for the occasional one there is the accompaniment of an outward manifestation.

By what authority can we dictate the method of entry? Surely this is God's business!

For myself, after many days and weeks of praying over this matter there came a moment of time when I was tremendously conscious that the issue was settled; to pray and ask again was an insult to God. There was the settled inner peace that, in yielding utterly to God, His Spirit had taken control to work out His perfect purpose. Emotionalism was absent, although there was a deep inner rest of spirit, and joy in the Lord, but nothing more.

In writing a letter to help a younger Christian, one of our present women students, just turned twenty-one, wrote these lines:

"This term I became so desperate in myself. Although I had a longing really to know the Lord and walk with Him every moment of every day I came to the place where I felt I didn't know Him as I should. I struggled to achieve a knowledge of Him for myself, but finally it seemed impossible to go on. The Christian life seemed too hard. Yet it was impossible to go back because I knew the Lord was real and I wouldn't be happy if I gave up everything.

"I was honest with the Lord and told Him I didn't even know how to get to know Him, and didn't even know if my desire was sincere, either. He caused me to read Phil. 2: 13 in the Amplified Bible—'It is God Who is all the while effectually at work in you—energising and creating in you the power and desire—both to will and to work for His good pleasure and satisfaction and delight.' When I realised this I knew I had been trying to live the Christian life in my own strength, trying to create the desire in myself to know Him better and go on with Him. But God does this, and I have proved that as I let go and trust Him, life is different.

"The Lord had to show me my sinfulness and unworthiness and inadequacy. He had to bring me to the end of myself; but He didn't leave me there. He revealed Himself to me, His all-sufficiency and His holiness, and then, as I let go and stopped trying, and let God live His full life through me, I found joy and peace, believing and knowing what being 'complete in Christ' really means.

"It is now a matter of abiding in Christ and yielding to Him (Rom. 6: 13, 14), and knowing His fulness within—no struggle any more, but perfect peace; it depends on the condition that I obey His command to 'trust' Him (Isa. 26: 3, 4)."

In creative faith, the secret lies in seeing things from God's point of view and boldly acting on the conviction we have of its reality. It is as if we have ascended with Christ, where we look down into a human situation from a detached other-worldly, other-principled, other-valued life system. Christ spoke from this position in the Sermon on the Mount. How could the meek possibly inherit the earth? Yet His teachings are more feared by the Communist world than any other's! When in the dealings of the Spirit we accept His values and start to live by them; when for instance we start thinking not in terms of career but of the Cross life (the Cross being the Capital "I" crossed out); when we start thinking in terms of how to give, rather than get; when ambition turns to abandonment and obedience, and the lust for security is replaced by the life of simplicity and sensitivity to God; when prayer is not an impossible ideal but a hard getting-up-earlier reality —then, and only then, we will start to see things with the eyes of Christ. We will have His values, His views, His vantage point. And then the will of God will not be difficult because we shall find that the Holy Spirit is able to confirm in our hearts the purpose of God for a particular situation. Should a phrase like "It seemed good to the Holy Ghost and to us" be confined, as an experience, to New Testament times only?

One local church in Tasmania was challenged through a message given in Sunday morning worship about having a "sense of direction" as far as its local strategy was concerned. The deacons conceded amongst themselves that there were indeed no unified, co-ordinated objectives towards which the congregation was heading. So they decided to have an evening of prayer and discussion, waiting on the Lord for His word to them as a fellowship. It came, with a unanimous conviction that a visitation campaign should be commenced in the vicinity of the church. Creative faith arose out of humbly acknowledging their lack of certainty and waiting upon God until the direction was unmistakably clear.

Creative faith is not for the carnal Christian. We cannot see God's way while we try to hold on to our own. In the final analysis, creative faith is a way of life to which we are shut in because of our refusal to be motivated by easily-available carnal alternatives. Real surrender triggers real faith.

We mentioned constructive fellowship as a part of discipleship. However, we have found that fellowship is only dynamic when those responsible for creating it are living in real openness and brokenness among themselves. In simple language, the students can only be helped in the measure that the staff are "walking in the light" with each other and with them (1 John 1: 6, 7).

Seeking to prepare a lecture one day, I sensed my thoughts were barren and lifeless. When I asked the Lord about it, a recollection came of an incident that had occurred several hours previously when, in the heat of the moment, I had used rather strong terms in speaking to a younger member of staff. Once this was put right, preparation was easy.

Details are important. The little foxes spoil the vine. On another occasion, at the completion of a lecture I inadvertently picked up from the lectern a ball-point pen which had been lying there before the class began. I had intended to ask later for the owner, but in the round of many duties it lay on my desk for a day or two, until unthinkingly I started to use it.

After a short time the Holy Spirit reminded me I was using something that did not belong to me! What to do now? Simply advertise it as "lost property" or be thoroughly open and confess to using it wrongfully? It was a hard battle, to share this insignificant detail with the fellowship and to apologise to the owner, but infinitely worth it.

Is this a scriptural pattern of behaviour? It was the pattern that brought revival to Kenya, and kept those who were walking in it faithful to the Lord all through the Mau Mau uprising. So it has stood the test of time and adversity, and, of course, it is true to God's Word:

"If we are living in the light of God's presence, just as Christ does, then we have wonderful fellowship and joy with each other, and the blood of Jesus his Son cleanses us from every sin. If we say that we have no sin, we are only fooling ourselves, and refusing to accept the truth" (1 John 1: 7, 8 Living Letters).

Surely the principle here is sensitivity—sensitivity to the feelings of others, sensitivity to the Holy Spirit as He convicts. It is interesting that the basic meaning of the word translated "obey" in the New Testament is "to hear, under," i.e. to be sensitive to the voice from above.

Constructive fellowship only begins with openness and brokenness; once these lines of communication are established within the fellowship, a vista of enormous possibilities opens up, because the dynamic of an uninhibited and united fellowship is tremendous. Take our afternoons of prayer-and-strategy. We all are completely free to state our convictions both in prayer and discussion, and through this very freedom the Word of the Lord comes to us. Our staff meetings seldom take long and can be quite hilarious, because all we want is to see God's will coming through, not the pitting of one viewpoint against another in hard bargaining for an intellectual victory.

Probably the session in which constructive fellowship is best observed is in the first session of the timetable, several mornings in the week. We start with hymns and praise (no prayer, or asking—just declarations of thankfulness to the Lord). Then there is an open time for any to share an experience, or a precious truth that has come to light in study or quiet time. "A" has been asking the Lord about a material need, and it has been supplied. "B" has seen a message in the Old Testament Bible School incident of the axe head falling into the water—do we have a "cutting edge" or are we blunt and ineffective? "C" has had the joy of leading a soul to Christ on visitation. "D" has had a letter from home indicating that her parents are becoming less antagonistic to spiritual things. "E" is hesitant, but frankly admits letting the Devil come in with fear in a certain situation. Could we please stand with him in prayer? So right there and then we take a stand of faith for deliverance, and consistent victory.

The Bible study then follows—forty minutes of digging into basic meanings, clarification of spiritual principles, promises to claim, parallel and contemporary situations to which the Bible truths can be applied, indications of Satan's activity, the technique of spiritual warfare, the resources of the Spirit-filled life, and so on.

The session concludes with intercession for our missionaries, a specific area being covered each day.

This has been the session that has bound us together as a working fellowship over the years. Not only do students attend; staff members, no matter the pressure within their own departments, make time regularly for this essential period of constructive sharing and teaching.

Humanly speaking, nothing holds us together. No staff member has a salary. No one is finally a boss (because all departments are subject to the total staff fellowship, and the whole running of the College is subject to the mission staff). No one need be inhibited from speaking his mind because of an employee/employer relationship.

The world wonders how we survive, and often church leaders are amazed that we operate without appeals and estimates and budgets and salaries. The simple reason is just love for Christ. Jesus said, "If you love me, keep my commandments." Obedience is the proof of the reality of love, and, when God has really called to a work and a fellowship like this, no one can escape without loss.

So then, what shall we say of these past twenty-two years, first in Britain and U.S.A., and then here in Australia?

Every year has had its own flavour, its joys and encouragements, yes, and failures and defeats, personal as well as fellowship-wise. But through it all, the momentum of service has been sustained by the intense conviction that, as a team, we are doing, through His resources, what God has revealed to be His wonderful will. The confirmation has been the flow of young men and women reaching the field and maintaining vital ministries in evangelism and church planting, worldwide.

These are some of the endless rewards and satisfactions of life in the strategy of God.

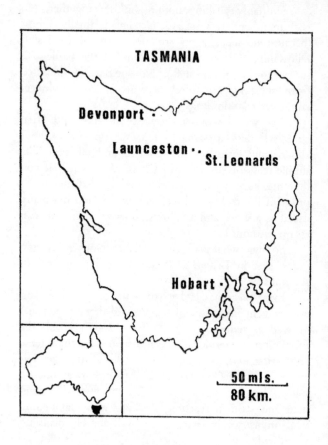

This island, one of the States of the Commonwealth of Australia, lies about 170 miles south of the mainland. It is 190 miles across at its widest point, and 180 miles long. The population, mostly of British stock, but with a strong Dutch element, is close to 400,000. The seat of the State government is the city of Hobart (120,000), and the second city is Launceston (60,000) close to which lies the small township of St. Leonards.

The island's history is a dark one. Convicts from British prisons were among its first settlers (1804) and the original inhabitants—dark-skinned people called aborigines—were finally exterminated by the whites in the middle of the nineteenth century.

The terrain is largely rugged, apart from the northern coastal and midland plains. Much of the island is wooded and large tracts of the south west have never been traversed by the foot of man.

The climate is temperate. Tasmania is known as the "Apple Isle" because of the large apple crop, most of which is exported in autumn (the northern hemispere spring) to Britain and Europe.

The currency is the Australian dollar, which at present is worth ninety cents, American, and forty-six new pence, British.

WORLDWIDE EVANGELIZATION CRUSADE
FIELDS

Arabia	Indonesia	Senegal
Brazil	Iran	Singapore
Canary Islands	Italy	Spain
Chad	Ivory Coast	Taiwan
Colombia	Japan	Thailand
Dominica	Korea	Upper Volta
France	Liberia	Uruguay
Gambia	Nepal	Venezuela
Ghana	Pakistan	Viet Nam
India	Portuguese Guinea	Zaire (Congo)

GENERAL HEADQUARTERS

Britain
Bulstrode, Gerrards Cross, Bucks. SL9 8SZ

S. Africa
8 Sutton Crescent, Durban, Natal

N. America
Box A, Fort Washington, Pa. 19034, U.S.A.

Australia
48 Woodside Avenue, Strathfield, Sydney, N.S.W. 2135

Germany
WEK-Missionshaus, D-6239 Vockenhausen/Ts.

Holland
Dunanstraat 30b, Rotterdam-6

New Zealand
15 Henley Road, Mt. Eden, Auckland 3

Scandinavia
Morkullegatan 50, S-724 69 Vasteras, Sweden

Switzerland
Hochstrasse 132, CH 8330 Pfaffikon/ZH